Mastery of Consciousness

Awaken the Inner Prophe

Liberate Yourself with Yogic Wisdom
Break the Limits of Mind, Body, and Life Circumstances

Tapasyogi Nandh

MASTERY OF CONSCIOUSNESS: AWAKEN THE INNER GURU

Break the limits of the mind, body and circumstances

- Brief Autobiography of Nandhiji
- Siddhar Yogic Insights into Consciousness
- Interview with Nandhiji
- 108 Consciousness Sutras

Invincible Publishers

First published in India in 2019

ISBN: 978-93-89600-14-8

Registered Address: 201A, SAS Tower, Sector 38,

Gurgaon-122003

Printed at Thomson Press (India) LTD

Nandhiji's Three Ariven Temple Visions:
Awake and Be the Yogi – World Yogi Day,
Mahasivratri: www.worldYogiday.org
Consciousness Community in Action: www.ariven.org
Global Consciousness: The Declaration of
Consciousness Movement:
www.declarationofConsciousness.org
Mother India: www.declarationofConsciousness.in

Nandhiji www.nandhiji.com

Mastery of Consciousness Experience/Teachings:
Kalangi Kundalini Yoga
SivaSivaa Siddha Chakra Guided Meditation
Music: Turiya Nada
Siddha Wisdom Teachings MP3
https://nandhiji.com/yoga-teachings/

India: www.Nandhi.net

From Nandhiji

My deepest gratefulness to my Eight Gurus who are my wisdom, inspiration, knowing and focus. Gratitude to the Precious Beings who supported me through this journey and made this book Mastery of Consciousness a reality! Najla Bose, Sri Prateeka Ananda, Rita Deepini Devi, Romarishi Ganganath & Tara, Lark Larisa Pilinsky, Jaigurunatha David Reed, Christine Dehlinger, Satish & Viji, Neeraj Wadhwa, Lori Tierney, Raghavendran Gopal, Brent Palman, Jesi Silveria, Anita Christopher, Stockton Smithy, Daniel Orth, Stella Diamond, Kia Miller, Richard Applegate, Catherine Granett, John Andreadis, Alejandra Salvado, Michael Garrity, Asheem Aggarwal, N.S.Shanmugha, Debi Buzil, Francis Olsen, Aghori Prajna Shiva Kalidasa, Linda Vanderstukken, Leslie Frazer, Yana Novozhilova, Vedik Shetty, Laura DiBiagio, Muru Arimugan, Jay Nair, Sita Siddhananda Leite, Patrick McCall, Carol Hawk, Suryadasi Devi, Darren Kramer, Ramesh Bjonnes, Aadi Brian G Zeck, Patrick Morgan, Dr. Clifford N. Alford, Charlene Christos, Chen Heng Ming, Aditi Capoor, Jason Caduff, Shreem Devi, Lisa Rittel, Tarun Adhithya, Eric Bhojak , Adam Jackson, Jesus Orta Ruiz, Thiaga Rajan, Teresa Kohler.

Preface

'In a time when so many are breaking free from outmoded convention and wanting to authentically connect with what is and how-to best be in a seemingly chaotic and troubled world, there is Nandhiji. I have known Nandhiji for over 10 years and know his story well; how he connected with the Siddhars and the path he has chosen. Few awakenings of this level and intensity choose to remain active in the world. And yet Nandhiji has embraced the life of a householder, visionary, entrepreneur, husband, father and author while maintaining a deep love for his gurus and the path that he practices with such dedication. This active engagement with the world is what makes the book *Mastery of Consciousness: Awaken the Inner Guru,* ever more potent.

'What makes me trust this book as an excellent guide for anyone wishing to Awaken is that in it, he shows due respect to all who have contributed to his awakening, shares honest insights he has come to, in verses of Yogic wisdom and Photos, and without promoting any path as exclusive—not even his own—he answers directly the questions so many of those who feel the urge to Awaken, ask. *Mastery of Consciousness* is not a quick read-through. It is a guide that can be contemplated and its verses like the I Ching used, when roadblocks and conundrums inevitably arise along the path of eliminating the ignorance, attachments and aggressive feelings–the Three Poisons that Buddha taught that are at the core of our suffering, that we all encounter. Nandhiji's presence lets anyone know that what he writes, he lives and what he lives, he generously offers in this gem of a spiritual guide. Beyond Nandhiji's wish to touch each and every one of you who pick up this book is also a platform for the Declaration of Consciousness. He invites others to join who similarly share a passion for awakening and transformation to a Peaceful world embracing the truth of LOVE.'

Robert Sachs

Author of *Becoming Buddha: Awakening the wisdom and Compassion to Change Your World*

and *The Passionate Buddha: wisdom on Intimacy and Enduring Love.*

Table of Contents

Section A

INTRODUCTION

Consciousness is the highest gift a human can ever aspire for!

In Tamil, one of humanity's most ancient living languages, a person who has health and well-being, financial abundance, spiritual blessings and a harmonious life filled with love is called a person with 'Yogam'. A person with 'Yogam' is a person who has been blessed – is Lucky. But more than this, a person with Yogam is the one who has been gifted with Consciousness. The path of Yoga, Yogam leads us to 'Ari' – to know. Ari is Consciousness – the Inner wisdom that awakens in each of us when in proximity with Source/Infinity/God or Consciousness.

It does not matter if a person has high or low IQ, higher Consciousness awakens a unique facet of genius/talent in each person. It is a gift that can change the way a person thinks. India's history of Saints points to innumerable examples of ordinary people transforming to Geniuses when awakened to the path of the Inner wisdom. Saints of all religions are able to 'Awaken' people, no matter the level of intelligence the seeker has, simply by shifting the level of Consciousness in the other. Consciousness can be described as a state of mind in which there is Harmony, Peacefulness, Clarity, Joy and wisdom. A conscious person naturally attracts abundant physical and spiritual wealth. The gift of Consciousness enables a person to have fulfilled realities and to be inspired at all times.

How to use this book, Mastery of Consciousness – Be the Prophet.

Welcome to your journey to Inner wisdom through this book!

'What an astonishing thing a book is. It's a flat object made from a tree with flexible parts on which are imprinted lots of funny dark squiggles. But one glance at it and you're inside the mind of another person, maybe somebody dead for thousands of years. Across the millennia, an author is speaking clearly and silently inside your head, directly to you. Writing is perhaps the greatest of human inventions, binding together people who never knew each other, citizens of distant epochs. Books break the shackles of time. A book is a proof that humans are capable of working magic.' Carl Sagan

This book is unique in its presentation due to its intent – to convey the Grace of Consciousness. This is achieved through Nandhiji's story; through the insightful questions asked and the answers given in the interview with him, it carries articles relating to the mystical pathway of the Siddhar wisdom, Yoga and Consciousness, and finally, by way of the 108 Consciousness Sutras, as each Sutra offers an important guide to absorb and evolve with.

The Consciousness Sutras elucidate the main teachings through each Sutra, along with images and their explanations.

Follow through each section of the book to reach the Consciousness Sutras in Section D.

Reading the Consciousness Sutras:
It is advised to the readers to read one Consciousness Sutra at a time. Mull over each by reading it slowly and meditating on it. Each Consciousness Sutra holds a special truth, like a nut within a kernel waiting to be cracked open with your own realization. Relate it to your own experience. Question it.

By understanding each Consciousness Sutra as a situation in your daily life, the wisdom of each Consciousness Sutra will be more meaningful as a solution, as an epiphany, as inspiration and a healing wisdom.

Using the Consciousness Sutra as your wisdom guide:
You could use this section as you would a deck of tarot cards, pulling out any page as a guide to a question you may have. The Consciousness Sutra on the left page will hold the answer for a question relating to the past, such as a relationship or past circumstances for which you seek a remedial perspective of wisdom. The Consciousness Sutra on the right holds the answer to a question related to the future, without reference to the past.

Digesting each Consciousness Sutra:
Please be patient with each Consciousness Sutra, particularly if you do not reach to the meaning immediately. Often, it is the special circumstances in life that give us the unique perspective that helps us understand each unique facet of wisdom for what it is. Revisit the Consciousness Sutra in a few days, weeks or months, and by that time because you have been giving the Sutra your mind share and thoughtfulness, the essence of the Consciousness Sutra will be easily cracked open. Much of our spiritual progress happens when we confront real life situations with Tools of Consciousness. The results from such situations form the core of our wisdom.

Absorb the Grace of Consciousness:
Write down, if possible, in a single sentence, the magical part of wisdom within each Verse as an Affirmation. It is an

Affirmation to the subconscious mind that transforms our bed of thoughts; our Consciousness.

Siva Be: Each Consciousness Sutra encapsulates the wisdom of 'Siva Be'

Siva means that we understand ourselves to be Spirits. Lord Siva represents the infinite vastness of ours as Spirits; the Holy Ghost. In realizing Consciousness, we understand ourselves to be the bliss form of wisdom.

Be the Prophet:

Affirm that you have awoken your Inner Lamp and you have access to your own wisdom of the Now.

The Prophet:

- A person who speaks by Divine Inspiration or as the interpreter through whom the will of God is expressed.
- A person gifted with profound moral insight and exceptional powers of expression.
- A predictor; a soothsayer.
- The chief spokesperson of a movement or cause.
- A person who advocates or speaks in a visionary way about a new belief, cause, or theory
- A person who speaks for God or a Deity, or by Divine Inspiration.
- A person who practices Divination.
- A person regarded as, or claiming to be, an inspired teacher or leader.

Aum Namah Sivaya:

Aum Namah Sivaya is the invocation of Lord Siva; Consciousness as Grace. When we say this powerful Mantra we are aligning to receive and be the Grace of God/Source/Absolute.

The images:

Following each Consciousness Sutra is an image that helps convey the meaning within the Verse from another angle or from a point of view that illustrates a larger idea in context. After seeing the image and reading the description, read the explanation of the Consciousness Sutra that follows.

Explanation of the Consciousness Sutra:
Nandhiji explains each Sutra in this section. You might wish to write down any thoughts, insights and questions you would have. There are interactive forums to discuss and attain more of the essence from within each Consciousness Sutra.

Read a Consciousness Sutra just before sleeping:
When you read the Consciousness Sutra just before sleeping, you steer the mind towards the Source. Your mind is then set into a pattern that is activated by that Consciousness Sutra while sleeping. Your quality of sleep improves, with reduced stress and lower REM (rapid eye movement). You wake up the next day well-rested and with a higher levels of Consciousness.

Read a Consciousness Sutra in the morning at the start of your day:
When your mind absorbs the wisdom of a Consciousness Sutra you begin to vibrate from higher levels, and each thought comes from a higher perspective. Each higher thought of Consciousness paves way for a reality that is more aligned to your heart.

Receive the gifts of the Consciousness Sutra:
When we understand each Consciousness Sutra, we realize the subtle wisdom ingrained within each Verse, necessary to be a Yogi. A Yogi possesses the super-normal state of mind - 'Turiya', the Consciousness state that the Siddhars describe as the state of Awareness beyond Mind. Attaining the state of Turiya gifts us with the 'Flow' – what is primarily needed to be the genius of life realities when we Awaken the power of Inspiration, Passion and Focus.

Your Daily Journey to Be a Yogi – a Master of Consciousness:

- Light your candle/ lamp at least once a day and connect to Source.
- The name or namelessness of God/Source is each individual's choice. What matters is the understanding that it is the default privilege as a human to attain union with Source/God and get Consciousness.
- Read one Consciousness Sutra and contemplate the meaning it might hold for you and the realities that align you to its wisdom.
- Feel the realization of your own Inner wisdom as Soul knowledge and your Soul as Lord Siva.
- Affirm that you are the Prophet, who is directly connected with the Source.
- Recite the ancient Siddhar Mantra – Aum Namah Sivaya – in acknowledgement that you are receiving the vibrations of the realized masters as your Master.
- Awaken more of Source union with joy and set the discipline to have more of this joy each day and each moment.
- Enjoy the higher Consciousness of mind to align yourself to your highest potential as each day's pilgrimage within.
- Be blessed in the effortless ease by breaking the limitations of your mind, body and circumstances.

NANDHIJI'S STORY

Brief Autobiography of a Siddhar Yogi Visionary

In Hinduism, Nandhiji is the vehicle, the Bull of Lord Siva. Lord Siva is Infinity and the Bull perpetually and eternally facing Lord Siva, Nandhiji represents the single pointed focus of the mind dissolved in infinity, as higher Consciousness. To the Yogi, Nandhiji represents the wisdom of the Infinite, the awake mind of Consciousness.

In this mini-autobiographic story, Nandhiji introduces you to his book *Mastery of Consciousness*. A full-length autobiography is being compiled by Nandhiji.

Nandhiji narrates his story in his own words:

'Having Guru Ayya as one of my Gurus and spiritually connecting to this Yogi, was dynamic evolving Grace. Ayya had been meditating on the Arunachala mountain cave. He drank just a cup of milk a day with herbs in it. He did not

move. He did not ever sleep – for he was in the super-conscious state of Turiya. After completing his meditative stint for 18 years, he came down the mountain to then continue his inner journey in his village, in solitude.

In his village secluded, Ayya's meditation is tapas- the penance of continual inward focus- for humanity.

Ayya is a Siddhar Yogi, a mystic rebel whose who attains his inner wisdom not through intellect but by deep meditation. The Siddhar Sages are those who journey beyond enlightenment guided by their ancient Guru lineage and grace.

My search for the wholeness of my truth took me to Guru Ayya and a journey beyond the mundane and the limited human experiences. It was like a deep childhood seeking being fulfilled as in having a Guru who was totally Source connected– and to connect to Ayya was connecting most directly with Source. Ayya rarely spoke directly and having a 'conversation' in actual physical and words was rare. But to those connected to him by way of his mantra, Ayya assumed the role of higher presence that guides and protects.

For me, Ayya was the ultimate spiritual treasure – I was passionately seeking the depth of Siddhar teachings from a Yogi who had attained the wisdom of the inner fire of perpetual meditation, that of Tapas.

To connect with Ayya, the seeker needed to climb up the Arunachala mountain starting before 5 am. Once every day, in the mornings, Ayya was open to receive anyone who sought him and he blessed everyone, sharing his ancient mantra and tea through a ritual of reciting prayers, although he seldom met anyone face-to-face through this ritual. This ritual was Ayya's way of sharing Consciousness as blessings to anyone who sought it, while still in perpetual inward focus of meditation.

I would go to Arunachala as often as I possibly could – at least once or twice every month. After reaching Arunachala, I would circumambulate (walk) around the mountain and then start climbing up the mountain to spend moments in the caves, seeking to be close to Ayya. On one such occasion, at 3 am sitting near Ayya's cave, I heard Ayya in the ecstasy of singing to the Divine. It was then that I realized that Ayya does not ever sleep; that he was living in the super-conscious state of Turiya, in totality of joy. Sages call the state of Turiya the 'sleepless sleep', or the 'awareness of awareness', the state of higher Consciousness. I knew this state of joy was like fire, capable of lighting anyone who was near it; I knew this was pure Divine Grace. (Many years later, I realized that Ayya had lit the joy states of mantra resonance in me. Upon Ayya's constant guidance to me to share with the world the Siddhar higher Consciousness through singing, my music, Turiya Nada, was created, with the debut album Cave of the Siddhars becoming a classic in the Chant genre of music.)

Each time I went to see Ayya we followed the ritual of prayers, singing Ayya's Guru's mantra and songs. As the mantra was recited, Ayya, his Guru, and the ancient lineage presence was invoked. The whole process was an initiation that spiritually merged us with Ayya and his Guru lineage. The Siddhar mantras given by Ayya are the roots to the resonance of manifestation, making every thought potent in its ability to create reality.

Ayya's instructions were then given by his caretakers: 'Go home, rest assured you have all of Ayya's blessings with you. You do not have to see Ayya face-to-face if you need anything. Please do not disturb Ayya.'

Picture: Up above from the peak of Arunachala mountain, sunrise moments from the Ayya's cave.

I went to see Ayya as often as possible, but even after three years he had not once called me inside his cave to meet him. I deeply desired to be welcomed into his sanctum sanctorum – deep inside his cave.

Each time I climbed up to see Ayya, I knew that a part of my limiting past was being dissolved by merely being near him, and yet I needed to know that Ayya loved me and that he wanted to meet me, the physical presence. My heart's singular desire came true one day, on my 11th day of fasting during the once-a-year Mahasivratri period.

At this time, I had taken it as my discipline to fast through the 14 day festival, drinking just water while focusing every thought inwardly into the meditative realm. I was in Bangalore. It was a spiritually-attuned early meditation moment, early in the morning, when Ayya came to me in his ethereal presence, telling me, 'Pack up your bags and come to the Arunachala cave. I am waiting for you.' My first response to Ayya was, 'How do I know that it is not my mind playing tricks with me and that you are real?' Ayya's response was: 'Ask me a question.' So I asked, 'Why do you sit in a meditative posture of Malasana that very few can explain?'

The Malasana posture is much like the squatting posture, a posture that is difficult for anyone to hold for more than 10 minutes. Ayya had been sitting in this posture for all his years in the mountain cave. (In nearly all descriptions, in stone sculptures and paintings of Yogis of the ancient past and Tibetan tantric yoga traditions, the Sages are depicted sitting in this squatting-like posture called Malasana, rather than the lotus posture.)

Ayya as an inner meditative voice told me: 'When a person attains awakening, he understands the body to be nothing but a container, like a shirt worn. As a Yogi, when I meditate, I am able to be the unbound Spirit beyond the confines this of my body. But, the Malasana posture holds me back inside the body. This posture encourages me to dwell more inside this body, to bring the light of Grace into my body.

'Secondly, sitting in this posture, I am able to summon all the root chakra fires up above to my navel chakra and master my hunger, the temperature of my body and my mind (as in sleepiness and being awake).

'Thirdly, through this posture I am able to regulate my breath and the energy of each thought. My left knee under my armpit stimulates left breath to go to deeper states of relaxation and my right knee under my arm pit stimulates my active awareness as the Sun energy.'

Ayya's answer convinced me, and a few hours later, I left for Bangalore for Thiruvannamalai by bus. After walking around the sacred mountain Arunachala in prayers doing the ritual circumbulation, I climbed up the mountain early in the morning. Ayya lived near the peak of the mountain where his makeshift cave was. I was surprised to see a larger than usual group of over 90 people around Ayya's cave waiting to receive his blessings.

Siddhars are hard to understand from our normal, rational perspective. They journey beyond enlightenment, and it's hard for a normal mind to understand the vast mind of a Siddhar – a mind that has grown beyond all comprehension to be expanded Consciousness. Ayya in particular is perhaps the hardest of all these realized mystics to understand. He could appear at one moment to be a mad man and the next a Sage.

*That morning, Ayya was beating himself up with a stick. He was shouting out crude bad words saying, 'All you ******* came here to see me for your own selfish reasons. What have I done to deserve this ugliness of your karma?' After a while of repeated tantrums and whacking of the stick on the ground, on himself and the tree next to him, a smile lit his face (from* *outside his cave, peeking in we could get a glimpse of his face). This smile was like coolness of the moonlight. Ayya then said, 'There is just one person who came here for me and he came here to see me for the right reason.' He pointed at me, saying, 'Yes, him – that's him! Ask him to come inside the cave.'*

Inside the cave, there I was sitting face-to-face with my Master, whom I had held, hugged, loved and shared every breath of awareness with. Now I was here, in real life, face-to-face!

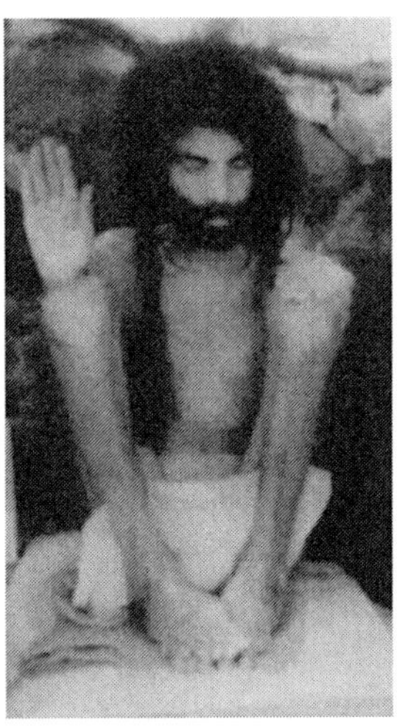

Picture: Rare image of Guru Ayya while in the Malasana posture on the Arunachala mountain during the early days of his meditative stint.

Now, inside the cave was another universe that I longed for. Ayya looked into my eyes. His eyes had the vast emptiness that contained all the universes. Inside him was the absolute nothingness that yet contains all the light. He looked deep into my eyes as he blessed me, applying his sacred ash on my forehead. He then gave me a new set of saffron clothes as his initiation. My mind just went blank and all I experienced was being a form of love. I felt his vast immense Being now reside in me. I knew this to be Ayya.

I climbed down the mountain and travelled back to my home town, Sivakasi. I sensed Ayya's beautiful presence sit with me and my prayer was – 'Please Ayya, forever, eternally, be with me and never ever leave me.' I was certain I carried Ayya's blessed Presence with me.

Early next day morning was the nearing end of the Mahasivratri of my 14 days of fasting. I woke up unusually early inspired, happy and joyful. I heard Ayya's voice in me say, 'Now get a paper and pen.' Instead, I grabbed open my computer and I felt a flow of words, abstract thoughts and a deep wisdom emanate from with me. I kept typing the words that bubbled out of me. At the end of the flow of words, a full 30 minutes of writing, I was about to write my name at the end, but Ayya spoke clearly as my inner voice: 'Sign below the writing as Aadi Gurunatha.' The name Aadi Gurunatha meant nothing to me, but I wrote it anyway at the end of the submission. The word Aadi Gurunatha resonated within me as a primal call of past lives.

A few hours later, it was time to drive down to the spiritual center of ancient India – the Kutralam, Pavannasam, Podigai Hills area – where year after year, I would spend my Mahasivratri night celebrating the night of Lord Siva. As we were driving along the road, one of my fellow pilgrims, a native of the area, mentioned a very old temple in the caves. He said that through the ages, the Siddhars considered this to be the most important of all temples and yet very few people had heard of it. I was happy to visit this temple, since most temples in and around the Podigai Hills area are powerful vortices of light created by the Siddhars and are some of the oldest temples of India.

As I entered the cave temple, I felt goose bumps all over me and a buzzing through every cell in my body. It felt like an intense home coming. I went right into the sanctum sanctorum of the temple and fell at the feet of the Deity. It was then that I heard the voice, as the amplified voice of Ayya, 'I am Aadi Gurunatha, the primordial Guru.' I slowly looked up and saw the small plaque below the Deity. There was the name – Aadi Gurunatha.

It was at this moment that I became aware of the ancient lineage of the Siddhars, and of my own births. The other name that Aadi Gurunatha had taken in his birth as a Guru was Nandhinatha. With clarity and loudness of voice, Aadi Gurunatha spoke, saying, 'You are Nandhinatha, the ancient Guru. Your birth as human is to fulfill our intent. Know that we are with you. Know yourself as Nandhinatha.'

My journey as a Yogi now felt unhindered with doors of grace open from this point. The name as my past, Adhipen, dissolved away and my spiritual name, Nandhiji, became more of reality and reminder of whom I am. This is one of my life stories that led me deeper into my journey to wholeness.

Picture: Fifteen years later, Nandhiji in the Aadigurunatha temple shrine. For Nandhiji, the story of Aadi Gurunatha and his own spiritual name reminds him of the enormity in importance of knowing his purpose and destiny in life.

Year after year, Nandhiji would go to this ancient temple shrine, sometimes by himself, but most times with fellow pilgrims. On each visit to this temple, without fail, a miracle would take place.

Nandhiji is currently writing an in-depth autobiography which will include the miracles that happen. For anyone seeking the Grace of the Primordial Siddhar Guru Lord Muruga – this temple is located near Tirunelveli, at the outskirts called Kurukkuthurai Lord Muruga.

In the beginning:

Nandhiji was born Adhipen Bose, into the Ayya Nadar family, one of South India's more affluent and philanthropic families. Nandhiji's grandfather was the founding father of the city of Sivakasi, a hard-working town known as the Little Japan of India. Nandhiji's father, A.S.C Bose, and his mother Kanchana Bose, were industrialists by profession and athletes by choice who represented India in badminton. The Ayya Nadar family were pioneers in the manufacturing businesses of matches, fireworks, metal powder and printing. The family also held plantations consisting of tea, coffee and agriculture amongst other varied businesses.

Ayya Nadar, Nandhiji's grandfather, believed that the only reason money was earned was for the sole purpose of uplifting society through charitable work. He founded AJ College, one of the A+ rated, well-managed colleges of excellence in India today, as well as several schools, polytechnics and charitable institutions, all run from the profits of companies that funded these charitable trusts.

Ayya Nadar was a satyagrahi – a non-violent freedom fighter. (The term was coined by Mahatma Gandhiji from the words, 'Fighter for Truth'). Ayya Nadar had worked alongside Mahatma Gandhiji in attaining India's freedom.

After India gained Independence, Mahatma Gandhiji requested Ayya Nadar to not mechanize his matches manufacturing operation; the initial process was labor-intensive, as the matches were handmade, and the factories employed and supported thousands of families. Bowing to the Mahatma's wishes, the family's fortunes suffered for some time, but the benefits were many – over two hundred thousand families owe their livelihood to the Ayya Nadar family.

Nandhiji, however, was destined to lead the path of a Yogi. Even as a child, Nandhiji went through the pains of scarcity in the midst of plenty. His paternal uncles had cheated his father out of most of his inheritance by taking over the profitable businesses and all the assets. Stuck in a string of court cases, unable to bribe the courts as his brothers did, together with the losses he endured on his businesses, all became a burden on Nandhiji's father. Throughout Nandhiji's childhood and into adulthood, in spite of being the grandson of Ayya Nadar, Nandhiji had to go through many challenges.

Nandhiji's journey into the Divine started when he was a little boy, sitting on the shoulders of his father while on a pilgrimage to Swami Ayyappa (a shrine in South India). It was on this pilgrimage that he witnessed a Divine event that would forever guide him through his life.

The pilgrims had to walk through 40 kilometers of forest to reach the shrine. Darkness had fallen, and they became lost, having taken the wrong path. While under the dark canopy of trees in the forest, there was doubt about being able to get back to the main pathway. And then a tiger nearby roared! Everyone was scared but they all kept chanting the Swamy Ayyappa mantras, getting louder and louder. Just then

Nandhiji saw a radiant being, as though luminescent, walking out of the darkness.

Nandhiji immediately alerted his father and soon, all the pilgrims felt a wave of comforting and protective energy, and there was no more fear. They all stood silently around this radiant being who was smiling. He said, 'So you all seem lost! Let me show you the way!' The radiant gave directions to the pilgrims who began chatting amongst themselves. Only Nandhiji saw the radiant being gradually disappear. While they all realized that the radiant being who had come to guide them was a Divine being, for Nandhiji, this radiant being was an ancient friend, waiting forever to connect. Through his childhood, Nandhiji knew that this friend could always be invoked by holding his breath whenever he wanted to. However, as a child he would often do what all children do – sometimes being reckless and constantly searching for newer adventures.

His parents put Nandhiji in a military boarding school in Lovedale in the Nilgiris, South India. Years later, while still at school, Nandhiji began to question many things, including his beliefs, his purpose and how it all fit together. Searching from a rational mind he became very practical and had a hard time with religion in general. He was a skeptic in many ways.

He believed in 'God' but he could not believe in the forms of Hindu Gods and their stories. He was frustrated with the belief systems that could not align to his rational mind. For instance, Nandhiji could not understand why anyone would worship an elephant-headed God or for that matter a Goddess carrying primitive weapons like a sword to depict violence.

Nandhiji faced bouts of extreme loneliness for most of his childhood, especially during his school days. He was bullied by his classmates and his seniors. He was beaten up by his school mates and on one specific occasion, he was beaten to the point where he permanently lost partial hearing in both ears,. In the evenings, he preferred to get away from his school and its activities and instead, wandered the nearby forests, away from humans. In the forest, he would sometimes build a fire to dissolve the feeling of immense loneliness within him. He knew that there was the truth that lay beyond his understanding and through the fire he felt connected to that Peace he so badly wanted.

Aged 15, Nandhiji attempted to write a book, entitled *God.* Every evening, sitting at the back bench behind the classroom, he would hold his breath for lengths at a time, seeking the truth – and he would be shown something about 'God' that he would then write. After completing about 60 pages, Nandhiji was suddenly unable to write any more. He realized that he needed a direct experience with God in order to proceed further. At that time, he felt that he so badly needed a guide, a Guru, a mentor, to guide him through the process to connect.

That which is desired with intensity always comes true.
Nandhiji's first Guru appeared when he turned 17, when he was introduced by one of his classmates to Lewis Parker, a 60+ year old gentleman from London whom he affectionately called Uncle Lewis.

Lewis was deep into the philosophy of India, travelling once a year seeking the mystical India for its spiritual wisdom. Nandhiji and Lewis would write letters to each other, Nandhiji asking questions of a philosophical nature and Lewis responding promptly with guidance for Nandhiji.

Nandhiji realized he had his first Guru to learn from.

Uncle Lewis with Nandhiji at the time of Nandhiji's MBA graduation in London.

After Nandhiji completed his college under-graduate degree, Lewis invited him to do his MBA in London. For Nandhiji, these were very transformative years. While he stayed in the hostel in London, Nandhiji would spend weekends with Lewis. Although from England, Lewis had much to share of the mysticism of India and the world, due to his own direct experience with Kundalini, the inner awakening. For Nandhiji, Lewis' presence in his life was much like a prayer answered, a heart desire of childhood coming true, where Lewis became more than just a mentor. He became one of Nandhiji's most influential early Gurus – one that would change his life forever.

Nandhiji returned back to India, and found that life had become inspiring and dynamic, full of opportunities, as he founded a hugely successful export business that was growing rapidly.

But life was to suddenly and completely change. Nandhiji's parents kept insisting that he marry, and it was during this time that a wedding proposal kept coming from one of India's most well-known political families. Nandhiji was hesitant. He did not want to get married into a political family or be in the public glare. He was told that Kanimozhi, the prospective bride, had an admirable nature and that she was a wonderful person, and so, reluctantly, Nandhiji agreed to a meeting. He met with Kanimozhi and her mother, together with his mother and sister. At this meeting Nandhiji and his Kanimozhi were given a moment in private to talk. Nandhiji did see the admirable traits of sensitivity, depth and beauty in her. But he felt marrying into a political family was not a good idea unless three of his conditions were met. So he told the bride's family the three conditions-

a) He and his wife would not accept any money from the family.
b) They would not enter politics under any conditions.
c) They both would be shielded from any form of publicity.

After Nandhiji mentioned these conditions, there was a silence in the room. Then one of the bride's family spoke, obviously a bit affronted by these conditions, saying, *'Do you know to whom you are applying these conditions?'* Nandhiji said, *'It is my wedding and future'*

One of them asked Nandhiji again, 'Would you be OK to live nearby Kanimozhi's mother's house here?' Nandhiji responded, *'My life is my adventure and I would like my wife with me. I could be living anywhere across the globe perhaps, based on what I do but I will not be living nearby.' Based on the reaction, he felt relieved that perhaps due to the conditions, the wedding proposal was perhaps cancelled.*

However, fate played its part. Nandhiji's sister and mother felt just after the meeting that Kanimozhi was indeed a wonderful, nice and caring person. As they had returned back to his sister's house by car, Nandhiji's mother received a call from the bride's mother saying, *'The conditions spelt out by the bridegroom are fine. This is the sort of husband my daughter Kani had always wanted. Let us fix the wedding date as soon as possible.'*

That evening the wedding date was proposed by Kanimozhi's family- within the next 60 days. His parents agreed. The rushed marriage event was happening like a mad dream for Nandhiji who was in a state of shock as little did he expect this reality and so soon. The very next day, Nandhiji and news of the matrimonial alliance was on the front paper of newspapers and in most magazines. The wedding was huge and monumental in size, as the DMK government, along with its alliance, had just won the central government elections and the state elections, and this wedding was an occasion to celebrate.

Upon the marriage being finalized, Nandhiji, who at that time was in the granite export business, took a conscious decision knowing that he was stepping into a world of influence, politics and favors. He did not want to be absorbed into all of this. He knew he had much to lose by this decision – to relocate his own quarrying operation to the neighboring state of Andhra Pradesh from Tamil Nadu, so there would never be a need to seek any favors from his father-in-law's government in any way. He completed the last of his trading to fulfill his export commitments before shutting even this operation in the state of Tamilnadu.

His quarrying and especially operations and exports from states across India grew exponentially. The initial years of a challenges in learning the export trade and lack of capital. That period was war like each day with intense travelling across India. When not travelling across India, he was visiting each of the five countries he was building his export business with.

His marriage did suffer due the stress of building a challenging business based on limited financial capital, risky trading of rough blocks and the constant need to travel across India and international travel for marketing.

Nandhiji often looks back at this period to offer gratitude to the inner Spirit who guided him to stay clear from the muck with a countless number of people approaching him for favors, deals and 'friendship'. Throughout his marriage to Kanimozhi, Nandhiji was pained by the enormous attention he was getting from businessmen, actors, politicians, 'old friends' etc who simply wanted 'favors' from him. Nandhiji made sure that he did no one, including himself, a 'favor' from his father-in-law's government. Some primal awareness guided him, even during this relatively ignorant period of his life. Nandhiji was not tempted in any way to profit or take advantage of his position either directly or indirectly from his marriage, even while facing challenges in his business.

The marriage did not last long. Kanimozhi wanted to end the relationship as she was not happy in it. Within one year of marriage, the couple filed for divorce as mutually incompatible.

There is a Divine timing in everyone's life to awaken as the next reality to happen. The marriage and the sudden separation felt surreal for Nandhiji, as though preparing him for a larger void in life.

It was during this void period that Nandhiji began seeking the Divine as life showed how hollow it was with the sudden huge limelight of attention and then the nothingness within life.

Then came the thunderbolt like news two months later. Nandhiji received a phone call from UK – his mentor/Guru Lewis had committed suicide. It was a big blow for Nandhiji, as all that he had learned about philosophy from Lewis did not make sense anymore upon hearing of the suicide.

Nandhiji went to London for the funeral.

In London in a world without Uncle Lewis, Nandhiji was confused and depressed. He was trying to think deep about Uncle Lewis and his own life as he sat near Uncle Lewis's bookshelf early in the morning.

Nandhiji was silently asking Uncle Lewis for a soul-searching meaning and guidance. Suddenly, in a room with no windows open, from the book shelf, a book fell down. The book was about Goddess worship. It was as though Uncle Lewis was giving him the directions to worship the Goddess. Nandhiji started his journey seeking the Goddess by way of daily prayers and pilgrimages, and he started enjoying the cosmic love- 'bhakti'. Life began to have a greater meaning for Nandhiji as he felt the devotional prayers and its joys.

A few months went by with more of a joy factor to cling on to but on the contrary to the joy was a growing primal sense of loneliness, the same feelings he had when as a child during his school days.

It was at this time, in the vacuum of the moment, that he met Lisa, who was then working with the United Nations at Chennai. Lisa was half Italian, half English. Lisa and Nandhiji were introduced to each other by a common friend. Lisa was a vegetarian and there was a natural spirituality about her. After initially dating each other, Nandhiji was attracted to Lisa's spiritual maturity. They decided to get married the traditional way of seeking consent of their parents first.

The parents on both sides agreed to the marriage and the wedding day was planned with the wedding to be held at the Marundeeswarar Temple in Chennai. Being engaged to Lisa did feel temporarily reassuring, although life was about to take an unexpected turn.

The Awakening:

The wedding day with Lisa now fixed, with two weeks to go, Nandhiji began feeling the vast void.

Now, at 26 and with the loss of Uncle Lewis and the sudden upheaval in his life, Nandhiji found himself standing on top of the granite blocks he was to export, feeling the familiar deep sadness and emptiness. Life just did not seem to have any meaning. All the business he did felt empty although he had just completed putting together a challenging large shipment. That particular day felt odd, as it was supposed to be a moment of jubilation.

Instead of happiness, it was a moment of deep brooding for no apparent reason. Suddenly at that moment, it felt clear. He felt the premonition of death stalking him.

Anxious and nervous about what his future held for him, Nandhiji went to a psychic friend of his to get a tarot card reading. He picked up three cards – and they all depicted Death. The psychic saw that Nandhiji was in a panicky mode. She told him that a great transformation lay ahead, because 'death' in the tarot card meant transformation for the better, and nothing else. She encouraged Nandhiji to look at the three death cards as a positive, life-changing experience.

It was simply not possible for Nandhiji to look at death with any degree of optimism. Death seemed really bad, accompanied by overwhelming fear and nervousness. Then, for the first time since his childhood days, Nandhiji began reconnecting to a higher power in the form of the Goddess. His choice to worship the Goddess at that time was so he could hold the Mother's energy of protection and love. He did feel the assuring rays of hope every time he prayed to the Goddess through a vast emptiness that seemed to grow each day. Praying to the Goddess, not knowing any mantra other than a simple plea of 'please save me' felt appropriate at that time, as he did not know anything else to clutch on to.

A few days later, while praying, he heard a clear loud and very masculine voice within him say, 'I am coming to take you today.' That voice was special. It was not loud – instead it was a gentle, firm reassurance of Peace and caring. Nandhiji had no doubts that the voice was from a Divine Source. That day, he did not leave his house knowing something was going to happen. He waited in the front room until evening.

At sunset, there came a hard knock on the door, and there stood a young person with extremely sharp, fierce eyes, with a radiant glow all over him. His name was Bhairavasekar Swamy. He looked into Nandhiji and said, 'Lord Siva sent me to you. I do not go to anyone's house. You have death coming for you. I was told by Lord Siva to come and take you beyond your death. I am to take you through this if you are willing. Would you like to come with me now?'

Nandhiji trembled as he told this young Sage, 'Oh yes! I have been waiting for you all my life. Take me wherever. Let's go!' The next day, Bhairava Sekarswamy and Nandhiji travelled to the ancient sacred town of Kalahasthi by car from Chennai – a journey of four hours. Throughout the rest of the day, Bhairava Sekarswamy made preparations for a night-long ritual.

He took Nandhiji through a deathlike experience – a revisiting of the death experiences of several lives before. He then gave a mantra and told Nandhiji to chant it throughout the process. In the beginning of the rituals, everything felt painful and eerie – the body was in pain and the mind was in turmoil, but slowly, the mantra recitation started waking up an awareness that was like a blue flame near the heart. That blue flame of awareness was comforting and Peaceful. Nandhiji knew the blue flame inside himself to be God/Lord Siva. Slowly the blue flame grew bigger and bigger and a boundless Spirit emerged. Nandhiji realized that he was this Spirit, the effulgent blue light. This Spirit, the Soul, was inside his body as a rebirth of himself in another layer of Consciousness. It was then that Nandhiji felt struck by pure light, like a million suns shining in him. The light was from within flowing outwards.

The next morning was a new life. Nandhiji felt as though he was a huge vast Spirit inside a new body as an intense bliss, joy and happiness that he had never experienced before. For the first time in his life, Nandhiji truly felt free. Happiness was experienced as waves of energy, being free, liberating, blissful and expansive as Spirit. He felt a light blue color of radiance emerge around his body and he now understood why the Sages also called Lord Siva 'Satchidananda', which means Awareness of Being Bliss.

From that moment onwards, Nandhiji's old habit of smoking cigarettes died. He no longer liked the taste or effect of alcohol. When saw cooked meat on the table he felt it was part of himself and could no longer eat meat. Nandhiji realized that everything he put into his mouth as food and drink was energy, and he certainly wished only for the highest of energy.

This change of mindset and rejection of anything that was not in vibrancy with Spirit was a natural process. The thought and thinking process itself had changed. It was a simultaneous transformation from within. Bhairavasekar Swamy had lit a lamp of inner fire within Nandhiji, through the initiation process through death to the eternal. This inner fire of awareness beneath each breath was Nandhiji's first experience of Consciousness.

Every day since, Nandhiji began following Yogic principles to re-attain the bliss that he awoke to. His spiritual journey had begun. Nandhiji realized the truth of his being as a kernel of bliss that was lit, and as a small lamp needing to be tended.

He spent the next few years seeking the wholeness and permanence of this joy that was set alight. He was fortunate to meet realized masters at every turn of his inner journey. These Gurus guided him. Going into the spiritual wilderness of South India in pilgrimage, meditating in caves, trekking into the forest shrines and learning and absorbing the age-old teachings, Nandhiji began to feel a sense of completion.

Meanwhile, his business had collapsed. Nearly anything and everything he called his own, dissolved away. For Nandhiji, the harsh realities of a falling business with debts that were accumulating and his second marriage nearing dissolution, proved to be an incubator for his spiritual growth. He went deeper into his spiritual pursuit even as every possession and reality dissolved away.

THE STORY BEHIND THIS BOOK – THE THREE SAGES OF ARUNACHALA

The wisdom within this book is itself dedicated to the Three Sages of Arunachala. Nandhiji was fortunate to experience this life-defining moment with the three Sages that he now shares:

It was eight years of all-consuming, single focused inner journeying through the spiritual wilderness, via pilgrimages, caves and daily Yogic practices, while trying to balance an active, external world. During this period, all of Nandhiji's external life realities as business and family had collapsed and was fast dissolving away. Life was a challenge for Nandhiji. He was hurt and pained by the numerous creditors from his dissolving business. His personal life was turning out to be painful and chaotic. His business could not support him anymore and his wife was preparing to leave him. Yet through each day of this war-like reality, Nandhiji was an optimist who lived in hope – he believed that only good will happen, and he nurtured hope that he would be able to climb out of the situation he was in. However, the hard knocks of collapsing realities led Nandhiji even deeper inside to seek solace and guidance of his spiritual path.

There were times however, when Nandhiji questioned everything that was happening around him; he experienced a tornado of destruction as he plunged deeper and deeper for the calm.

It was at this pivotal point in his life that the meeting with the three Sages in the Mango Tree Cave of Arunachala, a sacred mountain in South India, took place. This immense moment happened one afternoon after a tedious protracted pilgrimage that included walking around the sacred mountain the night before. Nandhiji was exhausted and napping in the Mango Tree Cave.

The Guru living in the Mango Tree Cave, Janardhana Swamy, woke him up saying, 'My Guru and two other friends of my Guru have come. All three Gurus have been maintaining a vow of silence for over 20 years. Tomorrow they intend to walk all the way from this cave in Thiruvannamalai to the Himalayas by foot. You can try to ask them any question you may have and they might answer you.'

It was like a destined moment for Nandhiji, as there were thoughts and ideas that he needed clarity and direction on. He got up and washed his face before going outside to see the three Sages.

Nandhiji offered his respects to the three Sages; bowing down, he said,

'Divine Swamijis (a term used to address men who follow a holy life), please accept my humble reverence and love for you. I live in a world of war and hard realities. When I am here and I practise my Yoga and rituals, I feel at Peace. But in the 'real world', my life is painfully hard and a challenge every day. Whatever Yoga and meditation I do, I still feel incomplete moments after I step back into my war-like realities. What form of Yogic practice needs to be done there in the active world that will bring Peace and abundance for myself and the world?'

For a long time, there was silence. The three Sages were seated with their eyes turned inwards – in an empty stare at Nandhiji.

After the silence of about five or ten minutes, one of the Sages, whose beard and hair was completely silver, spoke slowly in a voice of healing and calm. He said, 'What use is this silence if it cannot help humanity! I will break my silence to speak to you.'

For Nandhiji, this moment was like God in human form talking.

The silver bearded Sage began by asking these questions.
'Have you ever questioned why you left the comforts of your home, your business and your regular lifestyle to instead go walking around this sacred mountain, continuously doing pilgrimages, with no money in your pocket and living a life of a recluse?'
'Have you asked yourself this question, 'Who is making you do all this, who is beyond all this reality and why?''
'Have you tried instead to sit in the center of all this drama of life and asked your question to the one who is causing this drama?'

The silver-bearded Sage then continued speaking non-stop for the next hour. It was pure wisdom. Each sentence he spoke flowed like poetry, containing nuggets of wisdom as seeds of Consciousness planted. His words would forever be buried in the subconscious mind of Nandhiji. It was like a river that flowed endlessly as pure resonance that held little meaning at the time, but his words were like gems, treasure troves of deep meaning to be revealed at a future time. Most of what he spoke was way beyond what Nandhiji could comprehend and yet, it felt so profound.

After a while, the Sage smiled. Then all three Sages smiled together. They looked intently at Nandhiji for a while as though expecting him to speak. Nandhiji was in a daze and preferred to remain silent.

The silver-bearded Sage spoke again. He told Nandhiji, 'We are happy to have met you. We wish to offer you whatever you desire. What boon do you want? We can make anything come true for you.'

Nandhiji thought for a while. He knew what he wanted but felt the futility of asking for it. He laughed as he said: 'Swamiji, what I really want is not something you can actually give me. So what is the point of asking?'

All three Sages looked a bit offended. Perhaps they thought he doubted their spiritual achievement and abilities? The silver-bearded Sage said, 'Remember that we have been single-focused for many years. Our every thought is potent in realities as we wish for nothing other than our desire to be closer to God. Tomorrow we will walk the length of India with the singular thought of God. We are capable of manifesting anything. Just ask! Do you want to be the leader of this land? Or even, the world? Or do you want untold riches?'

Nandhiji said then revealed his desire – for the wisdom behind all the years of their silence. 'It is only this wisdom that I desire. Nothing else for me is of real value.'

Surprised, they said, 'Ask for something you can enjoy this life. You could maybe make a wish that you can use in your life?' Nandhiji repeated: 'Swamijis, the only truth of life and its realities is in the wisdom from where we desire and understand life to be. Your wisdom is the supreme treasure, perhaps the only treasure that is worth a whole lifetime or many lifetimes to acquire. There is no greater desire for me other than the wisdom behind the silence.'

All the three Sages were now beaming in sheer happiness. The whole space lit up, as though gilded by the sun. The silver-bearded Sage continued: 'We knew that you were a Divine child and it was for this reason I broke my years of silence. True. What you have asked for is the only thing worth asking for. Our wisdom is yours. We are always going to be with you as Consciousness.'

After having said this, the three Sages sat in a circle, inviting Nandhiji into the center, as they closed their eyes. Nandhiji's mind blanked out, for what could have been a minute or even an hour – it was impossible to tell. When it felt right to open his eyes, Nandhiji felt a light within. There were no more questions in his mind. Nandhiji felt whole.

The silver-bearded Sage spoke again. 'We are so joyful of this day. We wish to give you something that represents all of us. These words embody the collective intent of all the masters of Consciousness of past, present and future. The words are, 'Saivam Vetri'. Let your life purpose align as Saivam Vetri!'

In ancient Tamil, Saivam Vetri means 'Oneness Triumphs'. 'Saivam' means, the one who is awake to Oneness. It has several other meanings, including the realization of truth, Oneness, Consciousness, compassion and gratefulness.
Vetri is victory.

The moment Nandhiji heard these words, he was transported to his childhood, and an almost forgotten dream of trying to save all the cows, bulls and buffaloes that he saw crammed in trucks heading for slaughter. He would dream of saving their lives, creating vast lands of agriculture, growing food and feeding thousands of hungry people.

The Sages sat there smiling at Nandhiji as though they could read every thought running through his mind. It was time to leave. Nandhiji now was awake to his highest purpose as the seeds of mighty Consciousness were now sown with the words, 'Saivam Vetri'.

The Sages gave Nandhiji formal blessings by laying their palms on his head. Nandhiji had awakened the next layer of Consciousness and he awoke to understand his purpose.

Nandhiji's real life story had now begun. In fact, many exciting realities unfolded from that moment onwards.

Newer life begins in the US

Shortly after receiving the blessings of the three Sages in Thiruvannamalai, Nandhiji's Guru, Siddhar Rajaswamy casually mentioned to Nandhiji, *'Your Kali lives in California'*. At first, Nandhiji was surprised wondering how his Guru would know of California specifically. He knew however that he had a part of his life to be complete A few days later, Nandhiji received an introductory email with the title, *'Hi, I am Kali from California!'*. She was Najla Devi. It felt magical for Nandhiji as Najla could absorb the intensity of his email communication. Najla and Nandhiji established a deep bond by communicating to each other. Nandhiji then asked his Guru, Siddhar Rajaswamy about this relationship. Siddhar Rajaswamy said, *'That lady whom you have soul connected with is the Divine person I mentioned to you earlier. She did austerities near the Tiruchendur caves in one of her past life. You are destined to teach in the West. Go to the West and reach our blessings to all. You were in your earlier births from the West. You took an Indian body so you could learn from us. The West is your home. Go. Victory is yours!'*

Life's momentum was fast. Nandhiji visited Najla Devi in the US uncertain at first whether he was willing to let go of the spiritual coziness he had in India. It was his first morning in Santa Monica when Nandhiji took a walk on the Ocean Park Blvd. He was shocked to see again in actual reality the visions he kept seeing in flashes during his earlier years meditating in solitude. The vision was of the tall palm trees alongside the roads and the green gardens. This vision confirmed what he saw in his meditative depth as the place he would begin his new life. What inspired Nandhiji about America was the seriousness of yoga and meditation as a lifestyle itself.

Leaving India felt bitter sweet. In his heart he knew he was being lifted from our reality and placed in a much larger reality so to accomplish his highest purpose- to reach Consciousness to humanity.

After Nandhiji moved to America, his Guru, Ayya, would constantly direct Nandhiji through the meditative realm saying, 'Share with the world our Siddhar Consciousness through your singing. Through resonance, humanity will arise.' The music of *Turiya Nada* quickly manifested with the debut album *Cave of the Siddhars*. This became a classic in the genre of chant music and became one of the highest reviewed music albums. It also broke all kinesiology evaluations and was declared 'beyond the threshold of enlightenment'. Nandhiji attributes this to the presence of Ayya and all his Siddhar Gurus.

Nandhiji went ahead to then release his book Mastery of Consciousness, his Siddha meditation teachings- SivaSivaa, his Kalangi Kundalini Yoga DVD to reach Consciousness in its educative forms.

Nandhiji pursues his three Visions for humanity.

- Declaration of Consciousness Movement www.signdc.org
- Ariven Community www.ariven.org
- World Yogi Day www.worldyogiday.org

THE SIDDHARS AND CONSCIOUSNESS

A 'Siddhar' is a perfected being- a Yogi. Self-realization and the effort to strive towards self-realization has been the hallmark of India for several thousand years. India currently has an estimated 11 million Sadhus; ascetics who live by the charities and alms of others. For all of India's known history, the bedrock of Consciousness of India has been nurtured, sustained and grown through individuals whose whole lives are dedicated to enlightenment and the journey beyond that. Consciousness grows Consciousness.

For several thousands of years, the Sages of India understood meditation as the most effective technique to tap into Consciousness. After awakening to Consciousness, the Sages unfurled this state of focus, silence, contemplation, knowing and surrender further. These Sages were called Siddhars, or 'Liberated Yogis'. By liberated, it is meant that they were free from the bondages of the mind and the realities around them. They did not bind themselves to any form of dogma or belief, and instead chose experiential wisdom. Connecting to a Guru for guidance, they aligned with the ancient lineage of Gurus who paved the way for realms of a Consciousness much higher. The Siddhars approached wisdom through the process of 'Unlearning', which means surrendering of Ego, Old Beliefs and Attitudes, and old school Thoughts.

This inner journey of the Siddhars through Consciousness is called Tapas, also known as Tapasya. Tapas denotes an intense continued meditation practice over a long period of time. This could be for days, or sometimes years at a time.

In Tamil Nadu, as in the rest of India, it is common for an enlightened being to be called a Siddhar or Chithar. Chit in Tamil and Sanskrit means the Mind; the Consciousness. Siddhar means the one who has mastered Consciousness. When Gautama Buddha was born about 2500 years ago, astrologers identified his star of birth to be powerful in all aspects. It indicated of him as a higher being – and so he was named Siddhartha – the one who is a Siddhar, an accomplished higher conscious master. Siddhartha later left his home to seek 'Nirvana', the attainment of Liberation of the mind, and was then called Gautama Buddha. The concept of Siddhar is especially held in reverence in South India, where society considers accomplished masters to be Gods in human form.

Below is an extract of Nandhiji's own spiritual journey to explain who the Siddhars are:

Nandhiji was fortunate to have been taken through his near-death initiation to 'wake up' to the inner journey by his first Guru, who was a Siddhar master. After this experience, he began his journey into the sacred realms of the Siddhars. At each milestone came another Guru to guide him. A total of seven Gurus came during his journey of becoming a Siddhar who enlightened him to reach here. After years of inner journeying; meeting and absorbing the Siddhar wisdom; being consumed in the Siddhar Mantras while living in the meditative Grace of Siddhars, Nandhiji was inspired to write about the Siddhars from his experience as a Siddhar Yogi himself.

The term Siddhar has always drawn Intrigue, Curiosity, Interest and Respect in India. Whatever little has been known about them, other than from their Divine poetry and literature, the mystical allure of the Siddhars has created many stories and are often attributed to miracles and the supernatural.

While there are Siddhars in North India too, Nandhiji's reference in this writing is based on the South Indian Tamil Siddhar tradition, which is the Source of his lineage. The Tamil Siddhar tradition goes back several thousand years, to the worship of Lord Siva in South India by the Dravidians during the time of Ramayana, one of India's most ancient epics. Tamil is said to be as old, if not older, than Sanskrit.

The Dravidian clan, which spoke Tamil, was a well-established ancient civilization with deep-rooted spiritual traditions, worshiping Lord Siva and Goddess Sakti. What is interesting to note is that most spiritual words in Sanskrit and Tamil are very similar, with the only difference being the energy in breath consumed in pronunciation. The ancient Tamil language was the language of the Yogis who understood the practices of conservation of breath and the power of resonance. For example, 'sh' takes more breath than, 's', hence, in Sanskrit, one says, 'Shiva, Shakti, Mukthi'. In the spoken language of Tamil, it is 'Siva, Sakti, Mukti'.

The Siddhars follow the path of oneness that embodies Ahimsa, the life message of Mahatma Gandhi. Ahimsa means non-violence, non-killing, and tolerance and love for not only all of humanity but for all life forms. The Siddhar tradition is devoid of Caste, Traditions and Beliefs. God is worshiped as a universal entity. For a Siddhar Sage, Divinity is in form and formlessness, with the worship centered more towards a simple fire lamp, as a symbolic focus of one's own inner lamp. Siddhars prefer to call God 'Source', in order to free wisdom from the stagnancy of dogma.

Siddhars worship the Divine Feminine as the essence of wholeness. One woman, in the Siddhar tradition, is equal to nine men. She has the power to nurture and sustain life both within and outside the womb. Her strength outpours in the form of the unconditional love that she gives through her motherhood and by being the center of the family. In many cultures, including mainstream Hinduism, a woman during her menstrual cycle is looked down upon as being 'impure'. However, in the tantric tradition of the Siddhars, it is during her menstrual cycle when a woman is at her heights of Divinity, representing the energies of Goddess Kali Herself. With her monthly shedding of blood, she is purifying both herself and the world as the Divine Feminine. In the Siddhar tradition, spiritual growth and the inner journey through Consciousness takes place when the male element (our Spirit awakened in Consciousness – Lord Siva), and the female element (our experience in the body sparked by energy of Grace – Goddess Sakti), unite.

Siddhars from the practical sense:
In the pathway of the Siddhars, as we journey through Consciousness, we realize our mind being empowered by extra abilities such as envisioning the future, seeing the past of another person, reading the thoughts of others, etc. Due to the absence of Ego, the Siddhar Sages do not succumb to these extra powers of the mind and the super-normal abilities that awaken with the mind, connecting with the Source/God.

However, the Siddhars, realizing their vastness of being Spirit/Source in their ability to transcend the mind and the limits of the mind, bring this blessing to benefit humanity. The Siddhars bless humanity by way of deepening their own Tapas and gifting the guiding wisdom to all who meditate, as Nandhiji's Guru Ayya did and still continues to do so.

All realized Sages' advise to meditate in order to touch base with the higher Conscious Realm that is always there for us to tap into. Masters like Ayya provide a mantra to assist the meditative mind focus and connect with him in the higher conscious realm, utilizing the mantra so that our mind can align to the energized Vortex of Tapas that Guru Ayya is spinning in.

Siddhars by definition are those journeying beyond realization. Siddhars are not exclusive to any one region, as the ability to realize Higher Consciousness is a potential in every human on the planet. Such Beings are in humanity, spread across the globe, from all Religions and Cultures, as Healers, Scientists, Philanthropists, Visionaries and in various other roles–even blue-collar workers. Some of the Siddhars effect real changes for humanity, while others work on themselves in Solitude continually.

Some of the notable characteristics of the Siddhars are: absence of Ego, Compassion, Unconditional Love, continual Discipline to meditate and go within, self-realized wisdom, adherence to Peace and Harmony, and all that we can attribute to the heightened goodness of a Human. However, they are sometimes considered eccentrics and in some cases even crazy, since they live free from the judgments of others. Sadly, history has often seen these realized beings of Consciousness killed, assassinated, murdered and crucified.

To a Siddhar Sage who is living in the midst of humanity, the road beyond enlightenment entails living a life of Purpose and Focus. With the human merging with the Divine, multidimensional talents of geniuses are brought to the fore and action for the good of all comes to fruition. The path of the Siddhars is attuned, aligned and suited to modern day society, since they come to understand the power and wisdom of the Now. They choose to function in a society guided by their innate heart's wisdom instead of the rigid structures of belief systems of the past. The Siddhar path culminates in the colossal vastness of human potential, through the basic nature of Goodness.

This path of the Siddhars is appropriate for modern times, because it teaches individuals how to use daily life in order to grow spiritually, while mastering the realities that continually unfold. Every day can become a spiritual workshop! In becoming conscious, we become a Prophet–able to lead ourselves, and our created realities, based on a foundation of Harmony, tranquility and goodness. Our path then is to uplift the collective Consciousness of humanity. This raising of Consciousness heals not just individual lives, but also the planet as a whole.

Prophet Mohammed and Consciousness:
Consciousness is a key to leadership and its presence has led to power. In the midst of the battle for Mecca, Prophet Mohammed was calm and confident as he told those fighting

for him and those fighting against him, 'Touch your hearts and tell me if what I am saying is something your heart already knows!' Prophet Mohammed was referring to Consciousness as the heart's own wisdom within each one. His higher Consciousness outshone the then existing levels of Consciousness of those around him. His enemies were subdued and overwhelmed, as many joined the side of Consciousness instead of fighting. Prophet Mohammed motivated an army that had confidence in knowing that 'Allah' was on their side, taken up by the dynamism of his words and actions.

Consciousness however keeps growing. The sacred scriptures of the Quran were most suited for the prevailing culture at the time of the Prophet. Those were the days when unruly tribes constantly fought each other. It was normal that the revenues of traders whose caravans passed through those regions were plundered, or they were forced to pay protection money. These practices were an unquestioned part of their reality. Under the trying desert conditions came the added challenge of innumerable tribal religions, as well as the animosity of one tribe for another, sometimes lasting through several generations.

In those days, Prophet Mohammed's words stood out as the hope for Peace and unity. The essence of his teachings contains the same objective found in all religious scriptures– that of Peace. The new Consciousness of the Prophet unified people under a single religion and Islam expanded quickly through the Middle East and Northern Africa, as the desire for a Peaceful reality that every human could relate to was very strong. In fact, it was a primal need. Prophet Mohammed's wisdom and teachings contained more justice and Peaceful solutions than all the laws of his land before him. Of course, today Consciousness has outgrown itself over the ages, so that now certain parts of the scriptures of nearly all religions are considered downright 'Barbaric' when we apply today's standards of Consciousness.

Pathway of Consciousness:

This Peace was represented in the ancient Yogic pathway of over thousands of years in the Indian subcontinent as the understanding of Consciousness as God within each, as the rejection of violence, tolerance and honoring of each other's path to Consciousness and following vegetarianism. Understanding this Peace was the outcome of Meditation and Knowledge from within – the science of the inner world. Cultivated by the Yogis and nurtured by society through thousands of years, Consciousness and imparting Consciousness has historically been Mother India's gift to humanity. Looking back into history, we see Alexander, the Great come to India seeking a spiritual master. Many teachers, writers and leaders, including St. Augustine, one of the founding fathers of Christianity, recognized the wisdom of the East. Even the roots of the wisdom of Kabbalah can be traced back to India. Also, because of the vast trade networks throughout ancient India that connected the Roman Empire with China, Eastern wisdom travelled across the globe and influenced all religions in untold ways. These seeds of consciousness, planted by Sages over thousands of years, have now grown, transcending Culture, Race, Nationality and Ethnicity.

Today, with information technology aligning to all the Consciousness that has grown across the globe, we are all able to access this Consciousness with increasing intensity. Notice how many books there are today on topics such as meditation, enlightenment, conscious and Consciousness. We are at a major Consciousness revolution, having reached critical mass. We are the witnesses to this revolution.

Consciousness grows forever – it does not stop. When we are awake, the whole world wakes up. Within our awakened reality we understand ourselves as Angels having human experience, having broken free of the Body, Mind and Life Circumstances. Consciousness is the ultimate Liberator!

Siddhar teachings of Consciousness impact society. The truth of consciousness can be seen in a relatively unknown but important historic social revolution that took place in South India in the 1840's—Nandhiji's Guru's Guru, Ayya Vaikunthar, had set into motion the teaching that would usurp the caste system. Ayya Vaikunthar was a Nadar. The Nadar caste was similar to the untouchables, they were not allowed inside the temples. Ayya Vaikunthar taught that God/Source existed as a lamp lit within and all anyone needed to do to attain proximity to God and the highest of wisdom, was to light an external lamp and pray. By going directly to Source/God within us and circumventing belief systems to attain Consciousness, Ayya Vaikunthar triggered a social revolution. This social revolution unshackled the evils of the caste system prevalent in South India to a great extent, and ordinary people came to understand that they did not need a gatekeeper to the Divine.

This consciousness is now available for all, globally. Everyone can realize that we are each the Master, when we are liberated in wisdom. These are empowering moments for humanity when Consciousness is the birth right for each of us, where Consciousness is, Peace, Love, Harmony, Abundance, Wellbeing and Goodness of the Society, Nation and the Globe at large.

Section B: Articles

CONSCIOUSNESS IS THE ANSWER

[Ancient Tamil symbol of AUM]

Often, as a little child, Nandhiji would ask himself this question, 'What would you wish for humanity if you had just one wish to make?'

For all of his childhood Nandhiji pondered over the answers, as he realized that everything he could ask for, such as good health and abundant material wealth for every human, still fell short as a solution for all of the problems we face, individually and collectively, as one human race.

After waking up to the spirituality in his life and after spending years journeying within as a Yogi, and especially after meeting the Three Sages of Arunachala, he realized that the answer was simple; what humanity needed was not so much material wealth as much as Higher Consciousness.

It is the level of Consciousness that makes a person an ignorant sinner or a wise Sage. It is also Consciousness that defines the life we experience. If every person on this planet possessed higher Consciousness, then all limitations–such as Poverty, War, Hatred and Ignorance–would simply disappear.

Take for example, a boy of higher Consciousness who is born into poverty in a drought-stricken village in a country like India or Africa. One thing is for certain: this boy will not only survive, he will also find solutions to help others around him, mainly because he has a Higher-Conscious mind.

It is the natural ability of a conscious person to be able to think outside the box, to be innovative and to find solutions to break through the limitations of circumstances. To a conscious person, violence is neither the correct mode of operation, nor the right solution to long-lasting Peace.

Where Consciousness is, Peace, HarmonyandLove exist in the world; abundance and all kinds of goodness thrives. The values inherent and dormant in the human awaken and multiply themselves.

So, let's go back to the example of the conscious boy in the limited circumstances. That boy of Higher Consciousness would definitely not only break free of poverty for himself but will also come to aid the society around him. Some of the many historical examples of this include Booker T Washington, Nelson Mandela, Mother Teresa, Martin Luther King, Helen Keller, Albert Einstein, Isaac Newton, Abraham Lincoln, Albert Schweitzer, Benjamin Franklin, Jesus Christ, Moses and Mahatma Gandhi. This is but a short list of Higher-Conscious beings whose birth circumstances did not limit them. Instead, these beings transformed their own societies – and in the process, aided the growth of humanity to the shape of what it is today.

These masters of Consciousness have set a continual momentum of expanding Consciousness for every individual on planet Earth. Each of these masters delivered inner teachings with as much Consciousness as was possible for that time. They utilized many modes of action, such as political leadership, scientific innovation and inspired writing, in order to serve and heal people.

On a macro level, over the years, humanity's level of Consciousness has grown steadily, and moves today at a faster pace than ever. From Moses and Christ, to Abraham Lincoln and Mahatma Gandhi, to Nelson Mandela, and to the present time, to this 'Now' moment where we all share breath, the level of Consciousness has grown manifold. This level of work evokes a tough battle–these leaders faced ridicule, opposition, imprisonment–and sometimes even death. Throughout history, wars have been fought by Consciousness against ignorance. From the very moment humans ceased to be nomadic and settled down to grow crops, (all the way through history until recently), the pace of Consciousness has grown exponentially, as we now step into the age of information technology. Slowly but surely, Consciousness is prevailing over ignorance. From our history of resistance to change – particularly when it comes to changing our thinking – increasingly change itself is becoming a powerful social norm.

In many instances in history, however, Consciousness seems to contradict itself; as older wisdom becomes outdated. When this formerly useful but now stagnant wisdom has created dogma and blind beliefs, it needs to change in order to serve humanity. The perfect example is the dilemma the world faces now, as medieval belief systems struggle to change. Today, the written codes of law in most religions do not fit modern standards and requirements. The circumstances of such dictated rules of religion, as they relate to Consciousness, are not what the original authors and Prophets of religions intended. Society has grown and so has humanity; the honest intent of those masters of the past is now finished, much like driving directions when we have reached our destination. The uselessness of holding onto obsolete maps becomes obvious; our journey is now complete. So why do we still hold on to the driving directions and the map? Why can't we progress faster?

Change and acceptance is difficult for many. The newer frontiers of Consciousness are challenging for most societies, particularly where religion has been firmly grafted onto politics. The familiar, outworn sets of rules, however out of date, continue to serve the control parameters of rulers who often are tyrants.

This ignorance has plagued humanity, represented in crusades, jihads and repressive authoritarian regimes. Today ignorance is similar to disease within humanity, as in terrorism, corporate greed and totalitarianism. These are a few of the conditions of ignorance. Now we witness a world of hope, as Consciousness paves the path to creating a better human being, while we also witness a world of turmoil, played out as a constant battle as humanity fights against ignorance and lower Consciousness. It is time for us, collectively as humanity, to say – enough is enough. In the rejection of violence, and instead the movement towards love for each other, comes the flowering of Consciousness that we are all endowed with.

On micro levels, each one of us is witness to the speedy evolution of humanity, thanks largely to information technology, which offers vast amounts of information to supplement the rapidly rising levels of Consciousness we have already reached. This critical mass of Consciousness that is being voiced by many masters of Consciousness today is beginning to influence every human on this planet, directly and indirectly.

These are moments when we question our basic birthright and the most desired intent of each of us to be 'free'– but can we really be free? Can we free ourselves from believing every aspect of the Society, Culture and Religion we are born into? Are we free from the opinions of others? Are our thoughts a mere momentum of the past that are distilled through a mind that has been conditioned with limitations? Can our every thought be born from the 'Now', which then determines a crisp reality that is of optimal goodness? Is our mind able to step out of limitations and struggle and be the 'Now' moment, as did that master of Consciousness, the great and original being whom we call Helen Keller?

If we look at our past – at slavery, inequality to women, flat-earth belief systems and other absurdities –if we question these beliefs and flawed moral compasses of the past, we can then begin to understand how much we have grown as humanity since those times. We are beginning to realize the core teachings that all Masters of Consciousness of the past have known – that we as humanity are one.

Problems such as Global Warming, Terrorism and Disease are now bringing us together as we suffer from the self-destructive attitude of a few. We are now also more aware of shared information that condenses our global intellect and which has its roots in a Consciousness that belongs to all of us.

The rise of Consciousness is an unstoppable force that has now begun rapidly shaping our reality. Each of us reading this book at this moment is part of the wave of the collective ocean of oneness. This book, Mastery of Consciousness, has been written in acknowledgment of this time, in celebration of our unstoppable nature. This Consciousness has always been available throughout the history of humanity; in fact, it has been there for anyone who desired more of it.

The singular wish of all Sages and Masters of Consciousness was to gift Consciousness to every person on the planet Earth. This is the inherent desire in each one of us—to be free, to be Consciousness and to want the same level of experience that each Prophet and Master of Consciousness had with the Source, as this is the most profound state of happiness that can be attained. With Source Consciousness, the key to the deepest wisdom within each person awakens alongside an undiluted sense of happiness, accompanied by the experience of freedom and liberation.

There are a thousand ways to attain Consciousness; each religion and culture has its own unique way and each pathway to Consciousness has its methodology and effectiveness. Consciousness is like a perpetual bank account that grows with each meditative discipline and practice, with prayers and contemplation. The higher within a conscious realm a master is, the more potent is his ability to deliver higher Consciousness.

Throughout the history of India, the Siddhars* have been known for their ability to 'Awaken' a person to Higher Consciousness, either by their mere Presence, by way of Mantra, or by the way of Teachings. Their ability to do so is due to years of singular meditative focus and powerful Mantras, via their profound connection to their Guru lineage – and of course through the Divine Grace. Siddhar Masters are able to alight the inner fire of Awareness, to give the seeker a glimpse of Consciousness, through placing the seeker into states of Joy and Bliss. The seeker then begins the journey to wholeness, attaining higher states of Consciousness. The student begins to want more Joy and Bliss, and with daily discipline, over time evolve to be a Master, thus fulfilling the intent of the Masters before, to spread Consciousness to even more of humanity.

In understanding each of ourselves as a Master of Consciousness, we collectively can transform realities for the world and in each of our lives.

MASTERY OF CONSCIOUSNESS

As Consciousness grows, so does our ability to think clearly from a harmonious perspective, to bring focus to priorities and create the power of directed intent. These are certainly amazing and exciting moments that we share together. Many tools of Consciousness, such as Meditation, Yoga, Tai-Chi and all other inward-rewarding Conscious Activities, are becoming more and more popular. Because of this, our collective Consciousness is expanding faster than ever before. So, what does this mean for each of us?

Consciousness and its mastery are attuned to the word 'Siddha'. From the Siddhars, the insights of Consciousness may become the ultimate tool to transform our human limitations to becoming Angelic Beings.

1. Consciousness is Empowered Realities:
The manifestation of any desire happens through the strength of one's passion, together with focus and the sustenance of the underlying intent. Those of Higher Consciousness hold the empowerment to manifest with ease those natural Divine gifts, as they utilize the thinking process effectively.

However, greater than even the gift of extraordinary focus is the ability to see from outside the box. Conscious beings like Einstein attributed the ability to conceptualize beyond their mind to an unraveling of a greater truth. In the entwining of Joy, Focus and Surrender is a genius that springs from our heart as the most perfect 'Music'. Joy is Mother Kundalini's sacred fire; focus is mind's fixation to Source as in bhakti (Divine Love); and Surrender is the vastness of void that accompanies the knowing. The subtle essence of heart's music is wisdom—the poetry of the 'Now'.

2. Consciousness is Abundant:
The Siddhar saying goes, 'Lord Siva's favorite disciple is Goddess Laxmi and Goddess Laxmi's favorite God of worship is Lord Siva.' This means, when we are detached (in becoming Spirit), the abundance of that, from which we are detached, comes to us in ease. Likewise, when we are abundant (through the grace of Goddess Laxmi), we are detached. It is sad to see many spiritual beings suffering from poverty and actually swearing by poverty. (This poverty could be attributed to the vows of poverty they took during past births and their present attitude towards abundance.)

An oil lamp used on the altars of most households in India will probably have the name of Goddess Laxmi inscribed all on it. This is because when our lamp is alight, we can manifest a solution to any of our needs. So, when a Yogi sits in a cave to meditate and his body needs food, someone, somehow, will bring food. When Gautama Buddha was born, astrologers saw from his birth horoscope that he was a highly realized soul, so they named him Siddhartha. It was only natural that such an elevated being would have been born in the midst of plenty, as in a royal family. Where Consciousness is, abundance always is. Where collective Consciousness is, collective abundance prospers.

3. Consciousness is Freedom:
All poets, philosophers and writers throughout the ages share one common goal–that of freedom. This is the freedom to be happy and blissful and to embody the immense Spirit of infinite Consciousness. The original role of any spiritual teaching is freedom to 'Be'.

Unfortunately, Religion, Belief Systems and Cults have stood in the way of an individual reaching towards Source, by curtailing the freedom to be the wisdom behind the 'I Am' experience. However, Consciousness forever grows and the wisdom of our unique 'Now' of Consciousness is greater than any sacred scripture that ever existed.

The first freedom is freedom from our own Mind, freedom from Beliefs of the Past, and freedom from our own Karmic Veil. These obstacles keep us from understanding the vastness of who we are, that of Spirits having a human experience.

4. Consciousness is Oneness:
The Consciousness Christ spoke about came from a deep love that expressed Oneness. This love stemmed from the ability to see God in every human. Christ was way ahead of his time, two thousand years ago; his teachings were in direct opposition to the religious leadership of his time, which led to his Crucifixion. The deeper our realization of God, the more of God we see in all living creatures.

The first trait of a conscious person is that of compassion towards all living beings. When we understand the wisdom of oneness to not kill another living being, we will cease eating meat, so the healthy vegetarian food we eat will carry more energy to expand Consciousness. When oneness is found in life, we appreciate ourselves in all our differences, as one in many. We will comprehend the issues of Race, Gender, Sexual Preference and Culture. Our knowing will be more than just of tolerance. From oneness, the word 'Love' becomes more meaningful; it becomes unconditional, from the heart.

5. Consciousness is Purpose:
When we awaken to the vastness of the 'I Am' experience, we are reminded that our human body has a shelf life. The next question then is, 'What am I here on planet Earth to do?' As we journey through Consciousness, we come to realize our individual highest purpose–a purpose with Passion and Joy, even just to dream or think of it. Coming into the 'Knowing' of purpose, we attain the blessings of inspiration that enables Well-Being, Fulfillment and Evolved Grace in our life. Consciousness then becomes action and a reality. The collective reality of conscious beings in the world then creates heaven here on Earth.

6. Consciousness is being the Spirit:
Siddhar Kakapujundar, Siddhar Rajaswamy's Guru, explained the meaningfulness of this human birth by way of this story:

When Siddhar Rajaswamy was in the forest with his Guru, Kakapujundar, during the evening, many wild animals and birds would come to sit beside them as he and his Guru sat to meditate or perform the sacred fire ritual (Yagna). Siddhar Rajaswamy asked his Guru, 'Divine Guruji, it is truly heart touching to see all these animals and birds come and sit so Peacefully without fear around us. There is more to all this that I can see. Could you tell me about it?'

Siddhar Kakapujundar said, 'Angels are highly evolved spiritual beings, but they evolve slowly into the even higher realms, compared to humans, where evolution is quicker the moment Consciousness is attained. With the attainment of Consciousness, the conscious person constantly does good and evolves fast. Yes, of course there is much more to understand this evening from the Yogic perspective.

'Twirling around us is the Peace of ourselves and the Angels too. The animals and all creatures come to bathe in this light. Like all living beings gravitating to their innate wholeness, even the Angelic beings seek to evolve, and they do this by assisting conscious beings, the living masters. Angelic beings twirl around conscious beings, wanting to serve and guide the conscious Master. At the moment when a Master of Consciousness is meditating, all the Angelic beings circle around the pillar of light that is activated.

'When a conscious being performs a good act (Dharma) the Angelic beings also benefit from the merits of this good action. Through the Dharma done by the Higher Conscious being, the Angelic beings evolve. A higher conscious Master has many Angels serving them.

'The human birth and its evolution towards Consciousness is the reward that even Angels desire. Use this human birth for all its potential.'

Consciousness is the awake awareness of being a Spirit but having a human experience. The Spirit is the 'We, the many as One'. This inner wisdom explains how spiritual beings have legions of Angelic beings as well as the Source serving them to attain the highest aspiration for humanity. This Spirit as experience is our own inner bliss of being in the 'Now'.

NINE JEWELS OF YOGA: SIDDHAR WISDOM, THE TANTIRAM

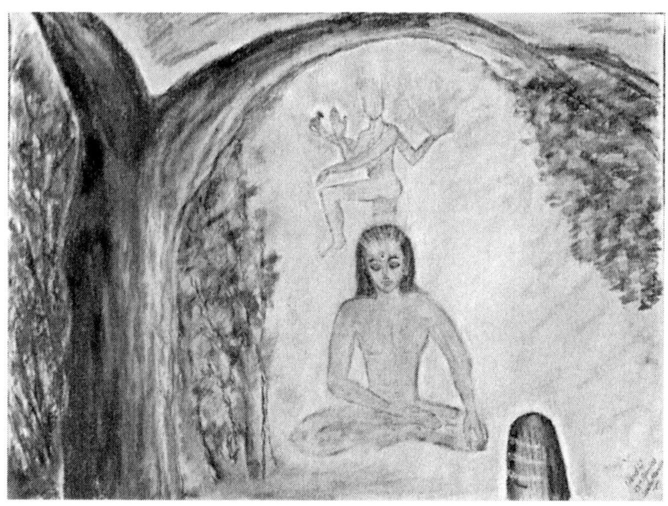

From the mystical depths of yoga come the secretive teachings of 'Tantiram'– the roots to Yoga and Tantra.

Traditionally, these teachings were held within an inner circle, primarily to be shared only with those who were spiritually mature enough to handle the vast, potent energies of the awakened Mother Kundalini.

Today, Yoga is known as a form of exercise and practice undertaken to reach awareness. But, here, it is necessary to understand Yoga and its practice from the perspective of the Siddhar Sages.

1. Yogic practice enables us to Meditate all day.
The purpose behind our daily discipline of yoga is to find total union with the Source, to unite with each moment in supreme Peace, to find the Harmony within, the calm center, (starting

with a little practice as the first step). In other words, we do yoga to attain a state of perpetual meditation.

2. Yoga is tantra.
The union of human with the Source through the sacredness of the 'orgasm' is Tantiram. Tantra comes from the word Tantiram, the ancient wisdom of the realized to magnify human realities to their highest purpose – to realize the orgasmic joys of being on every level of human reality that represents all the Seven Chakras.

All Hatha yoga is Tantra. Each layer of reality, starting from the roots of sensuality to the leaves of active doing, has a state of joy which grows from the limited to the unlimited. When we are in this 'Flow' we are blessed by an inspired life and its abundant reality.

3. Yoga is the realization of the Source in all things – 'Tat Vam Asi'– meaning: 'That Thou Art'. However, to understand Tat Vam Asi as an actual experience as a Yogi, we need to understand that we contain all facets of the Infinite and the Finite, which are represented by the five elements.

The Yogi connects to each of the five elements to be one. Within this mystical wisdom is the practice of 'tumo'– the ability to generate heat from within, and to go beyond the limits of heat and cold. The practice of integrating with the five elements allows a Yogi to be the master of the 'Now' in the natural environment.

The five elements are:
1. Earth — our body
2. Water/Fluidity — our mind
3. Fire — our intelligence and the intelligence of life
4. Air — our breath/air and the wisdom of Life, Force and Prana
5. The eternal Source, Space and Void — to awaken to being the dance within the Void is to be Lord Siva, the Spirit.

Through our daily yoga, when we find union with Source through the five elements, we realize oneness as the experience of being thc All.

4. Yoga is the celebration of our body as a sacred shrine and the genius of the mind that enshrines our spirit.
Yoga naturally induces good health. A healthy body allows the mind to focus on higher ideals, such as devotion and union with Source. However, our daily practice of yoga is beyond just health and well-being. Connecting the mind to Source awakens the genius within ourselves — the amazing unique potency each of us is gifted with from birth. By connecting the body to Source, we awaken to rejuvenating youthful energies.

5. Within each yoga posture is a treasured facet of empowerment.
Each yoga posture has a specific effect on our external reality. For instance, the warrior posture helps better focus our thoughts. The downward dog posture enhances mindfulness, taking us towards the surrender of the mind, the past and our thoughts, into the calm Harmony of the center, by way of breath and stillness; this awakens the underlying energy within each posture. To rest in the absolute state of Harmony within each posture is to attain the tranquility of breath, 'Sthira'. Yoga is much like shooting to the stars and then coming back home to the ocean of tranquility through each posture.

6. To practice yoga is to be on the path of liberation.
The mind is conditioned by many things – the past, the karmic imprints that limit us, and also beliefs which stop us from realizing that we are Source itself. To realize the One within ourselves that is in Harmony, love, Peace, happiness, bliss and oneness, is to be God/Source. The objective of yoga is to climb above the mind and thoughts to the state of being Spirit — directly experiencing Source as the sacred silence. When we awaken to realize ourselves as the Spirit, beyond the mind

and the chatter of thoughts, we appreciate Source in all the pathways of religion. And yet, we are not confined by restrictive religious limitations. A Yogi is a Prophet directly experiencing Source.

7. A Yogi is disciplined for a good reason.
When we experience the intense joys of yoga via bliss, expansiveness and a sense of freedom, health and Harmony, we take an intent to have this joy every day. When we do yoga regularly, we step out of the confines of a regular 24 hour day, differentiated between daytime and nighttime, and the ups and downs of the mind; instead, yoga awakens us to step into the higher conscious state of 'Turiya'— the sleepless sleep — the super-mind that enables us to accomplish far more than normally possible. In being disciplined, a Yogi sets himself/herself free.

8. In yoga we ride the breath of a river of Consciousness.
Through the left breath, the Moon energies and the right breath, the Sun energies, a Yogi rides through Consciousness with awareness.

9. Yoga is attainment of fulfillment in life — the Yogam.
'Yogam' means wholeness. Yogam is used today colloquially in Tamil to describe being lucky in all respects. To do yoga is to be lucky and favored in all aspects of love. From health, love and career, to the spiritual journey, yoga is an effective tool. When Yogis face a crisis in life, having a higher conscious perspective usually enables them to look at the crisis as an opportunity. Finding wholeness in ourselves from the inner joys that are not really dependent on external realities, we are able to create a life of wholeness that is complete in all its goodness.

THE SECRETS WITHIN YOGA

The gift of grace comes from having a daily discipline to attain higher Consciousness, health, abundance and love. Yoga naturally yields all attributes of yogam (luck). These are precious moments for humanity, as higher Consciousness is now a reality. Yoga, in the Western sense spearheads this awakening, even if it is considered a simple exercise for health benefits and fashion, instead of a spiritual discipline; the taste of a drop of honey will eventually lead to the honey pot of higher Consciousness.

The Siddhar wisdom is potent when applied to the practice of yoga, as the body is an effective tool to lead the mind towards the inner core of realization. By yoga we refer to 'Hatha' yoga as practiced in the West – the sequence of physical postures and the inner journey created through this practice. We recommend utilizing the traditional Sun Salutation* sequence to experience the teachings below. Ideally, the Sun Salutation by itself is sufficient to attain core Consciousness, which is the objective of our Yogic practice.

Below are some insights of Kalangi Kundalini Yoga, the yoga of the Sages:

1. Yoga is a Journey through Breath and Consciousness.
'Ha' and 'Tha' of Hatha yoga means the intertwining of Sun and Moon energies of the breath. Hatha yoga is in reality the journey of Consciousness through breath. The right breath is the Sun and the left breath is the Moon. The Sages call these two breath streams the inner rivers through which we ride through awareness. By being aware of our breath in its Sun and Moon energy, we are able to utilize the natural currents within breath via yoga. To swim along with the predominant breath and to stimulate the Sun breath and the Moon breath equally enables us to flow with the inner currents of the mind and Consciousness. To know breath and the Source of breath

is to know life, death and the immortal Spirit. Harnessing breath, we awaken to the wisdom of being Spirit.

2. Awakening Energies of Gratitude:
Our Consciousness begins from each cell; each cell owes its existence to our parents – to Father and Mother. The initial step of awakening body Consciousness is to acknowledge our Father and Mother in gratitude. Through the first round of Sun Salutation, we utilize the asana sequence of the left to visualize and express gratitude to our Mother – the Moon breath. Likewise, we utilize the sequence of the right to visualize and express gratitude to our Father – the Sun breath. By acknowledging our Father and Mother (as in thought, dedication and gratitude) who are the seeds that created our body, and who are part of the thinking process we possess, we shift our body Consciousness field of energy. When we are thankful and grateful to our parent's unconditional love from the moment of our birth, we are able to vitalize every cell of our body to a state of wellbeing.
Our first initiation towards higher Consciousness begins with Gratitude. Gratitude and coming to terms with body Consciousness paves the way to 'Now' – this is where the yoga practice begins.

3. Activate the Root Chakra & Invoke Lord Ganesh's Blessings:
Lord Ganesh, the essence of the root chakra, is invoked in the beginning of all endeavors to enable success. The success of the inner journey, Kundalini awakening and higher Consciousness, relates to the strength and power of the root chakra. The root chakra, once activated through yoga, holds the key to the wellbeing of the body in physical reality, as well as in the spiritual essence, and this creates a strong foundation of Harmony for awakening Mother Kundalini. The root chakra (the muladhara) needs to be activated through the bandha (the inner lock, called the mulabandha), visualization and mantra. The muladhara is where the Inner lamp is. When we light this inner lamp through our daily yoga practice, not

only do we awaken the Kundalini energy, but we are also taken through our inner journey safely, because we have been blessed by Ganesh. In practice, the mulabandha that awakens the root chakra is easily activated through the Sun Salutation process.

4. Invoke Our Gurus Through Yoga:
When we understand breath as a tool to Consciousness, we realize the space beyond breath as infinite wisdom, the Guru. In yoga, as we journey through Consciousness and states beyond the mind, the awareness beyond the mind is the Guru who continues to guide us. Each thought carries energy and thoughts of our Guru in the physical or spiritual form which carries expanded energies of wisdom. When we invoke Christ or Babaji or our personal Gurus to guide us through our Yogic journey, we are guided through a higher wisdom connection that is fulfilling and nourishing; this is the next level of Consciousness. Guru Consciousness is activated from the chakra above the navel, which the Yogis call the Guru Chakra (not described in any textbooks or intellectual teachings of yoga). Tapping into this energy field just above the navel, we access vast unlimited energy even as we awaken to the primal wisdom of Higher Consciousness. Yogis activate the Guru Chakra to climb above Consciousness, to gain the freedom to exist beyond hunger, heat/cold and sleep/tiredness. When we realize that the Guru is Kundalini and the Kundalini is a state of Consciousness, we are the Guru.

5. Yoga with Mantra Is Effective:
The mind and thoughts are vibrations. Mantras are a vibration-inducing resonance that shift and transform the frequency of the mind in order to generate thoughts that are more aligned to the energy within the mantra – this is done through breath. When we recite mantras through our Yogic sequences, our breath entwines with the mantra to unravel the higher energies of Consciousness within the mantra.
Each chakra or energy center is activated through the mantras, through breath and through our awareness, allowing us to

kindle and ride Mother Kundalini. Awakening our inner fire, the Kundalini, we utilize our daily yoga to transform ourselves. Riding on Kundalini as a state of Consciousness while going through the sequences of yoga, we evolve from human to Angelic. When we do yoga simply as a physical exercise without awareness of the sacredness of breath, we are more likely to injure our body and not receive the amazing and beautiful benefits of real yoga.

6. The Special Universal Cave – Third Eye:
All rituals and disciplines finally lead to the supreme state of being still – the attainment of vibrant stillness of meditation. This vibrant stillness within happens when we find our center. By practicing yoga, we awaken the inner fires of Kundalini that is experienced as surging joy and bliss that leads to vibrant stillness.

This surge of bliss initially is like a nuclear explosion rushing above the crown chakra. A Yogi directs the explosive energies of the crown chakra towards the third eye to harmonize this inner fire with focus. This third eye focus takes us to the seat of the Universe – the magical space that is the meeting point of Source and human. Awakening the vast energies within ourselves through breath, asana and the grace of mantra, we rise to the seat of Consciousness, to the third eye. The third eye is the experience of conscious samadhi – a state of awareness that exists while being absorbed in meditative oneness. In bringing all the focus through the third eye, we deploy the Kundalini energies of bliss, manifested as the wisdom and super-normal strength in our physical realities. The objective of yoga is the attainment of being Spirit having a human experience, or in practical terms, to be able to bring Source energy into physical realities.

Much of the Hatha yoga styles we have in the West are beautiful hybridizations of the traditional yoga practiced in India, but with a focus on the needs of pro-active individuals and directed more towards the body.

Ever-expanding Consciousness is pure wisdom that is reflected in the present moment. As there is truth in the dynamic nature of ever-expanding Consciousness of the present moment, there is truth in the hybridization of yoga, as long as the yoga practice is in tune with uniting the Source to our human experience via Yogic principles. The spiritual end of experience that aligns with the stillness of the mind and the vastness of being Spirit is beyond scriptures and belief systems in its truth.

From the perception of the Siddhar Sages who live the life of yoga in its entirety, the yoga journey is about being liberated as Spirit, and then taking care of the body, understanding that the body is a shrine that holds the divinity of Self. As we are liberated from the mind and body to know ourselves as Spirit, and then knowing the body as a shrine in which we experience the mind as a tool of Consciousness, the inner journey through Yogic wisdom unfolds each day as life-enhancing experiences.

7. Five Elements and Yoga:
Key to understanding Hatha yoga is the realization of the vastness of our Spirit and its natural impulse toward awakening, and the knowledge that the human body is a shrine. The Yogi understands that the human body contains all of the Universe and Mother Earth. This 'all-ness' is contained in the five elements — in earth, water/fluidity, fire, air and void/space/infinity.

The Yogi understands the divinity within each of the five elements. Each element represents the totality of the universe. Once this is understood mastery of Consciousness is attained. So in our daily yoga, awareness of our inner journey through the elements paves the way toward the mastery of wholeness.

The five elements as described by Yogic philosophy are known as the 'pancha bhoota'. The body is represented as the earth element. Water/fluidity represents the life force and our intellect. The fire element represents all the various 'fires' within our body, from digestion to the thinking process. The air element represents our breath, the air we breathe and the energy within the breath, our prana. The infinite void element is our experience of the meditative state of the 'mind beyond mind' state. The experience of the element of infinity is bliss and joy. The element of infinity is our direct experience of the Spirit that we are.

8. Do Yoga Nude (only when or if possible!)
While the idea of practicing yoga in the nude may sound alarming, for a Yogi, wearing the minimal clothing means wearing the entire infinite sky as clothes. Digambara, the sky-clad one, is another name for Lord Siva, the supreme Yogi. Practicing yoga in the nude enables us to integrate the five elements as one body, one being.

From the Yogic experience, and through grace and learning, comes the ability of the mind/body to break free of all limits and rise above extreme cold or heat, hunger and sleep. The concept of 'tumo', the inner fire that produces warmth for the body is a vital aspect of our Yogic journey. By practicing yoga in the nude, we integrate the five elements.

How to practice nude yoga:

- If you are indoors, open your window or door to keep the outside air flowing inside, so you remain connected with the air element.
- Be conscious of the temperature (hot or cold) and allow your Yogic practice to generate the inner fires that work like a thermostat to equalize the indoors with the outdoors.
- Allow your awareness to go beyond the mind to connect with the infinite nature of the sky. Realizing that we are infinite beings doing yoga is the rich experience of the Spirit having a human experience.

9. The Power Within Each Posture — Sthira:
Sthira is the attainment of calm, tranquil, Harmony of the breathless breath in-breath. The Himalayan Master, Mahavatar Babaji taught that sthira can be attained through yoga and meditation, and that within each posture is the trigger of vital energies kindled through breath. (For those who have not read this wonderful book, a great life-changing gift of reading awaits you!) From Mahavatar Babaji comes the mystical kriya yoga which embodies the essence of 'sthira' as a very vital part of the practice.

Through each posture, dive into this tranquil space by utilizing the breath of sthira and expand the 'self'. This 'self' is our awareness of our vast being-ness that is also experienced through the recitation of 'AUM'. Sthira is the attainment of bliss and joy through breath from the breathless being. A yoga session without reciting 'AUM' is glorified gymnastics and presents much danger since we are not including the greatness of our partnership with Source. In the breath of sthira is the realization of the eternal AUM that makes us aware of our infinite being, one with Source.

10. The Yogic Journey Includes Skipping/Dancing/Running:
The yoga practice we do comes originally from the Sages who lived in the wilderness of caves and mountains in India. Every day they walked, climbing up hillocks and hills. Most temples and shrines in India are located up in the hills to facilitate such pilgrimages. Their daily Hatha yoga practice complemented their walking, and their food intake was minimal or optimal.

In our society we consume far more calories than we need. We are exposed to huge blasts of stress energies. We live without the need to walk on a daily basis. We can transcend this environment by including skipping and/or dancing and/or running and/or cycling alongside our daily yoga practice. I recommend including any additional activity that gives more of joyfulness, as joy paves the way to daily discipline.

11. Do Your Own Daily Yoga:
Utilize a yoga studio as you would use a walking stick. Yoga studios are for us to learn sequences of asanas, but this is not a substitute for your daily yoga practice. Your daily yoga practice with or without a yoga studio is important for your daily inner journey in its practice, learning, wisdom and experiences.

There is a deeper wisdom that stems from the Yogic perception of time. When we commit to our own daily practice that does not rely on anyone else or other circumstances (such as a yoga studio), we begin to step into a realignment of our 24 hour cycle through the gift of yoga — that of timelessness. Practicing yoga is a powerful form of worship and a journey into timelessness. Each day consists of 24 hours of day/night time that limits us. When we step into timelessness just once a day through yoga, we reflect life as though we are the Sun; the Sun does not experience night or day, and so the mind ceases to be limited by the perception of diurnal change.

Another key benefit of having our own daily yoga practice is in awakening ourselves to be the greatest master and the most deserving student. When we learn from a yoga teacher, we are then like a sponge, able to incorporate all the gold nuggets of wisdom into our daily practice.

12. Yoga is Tantra:
Tantra comes from the pre-vedic teachings of South India, from the Dravidians. The worship of Lord Siva and Goddess Sakti and its associated Yogic teachings was called 'Tantiram', the roots of tantra. Tantiram is to unite Source with our human reality through the wisdom of joyfulness. Tantiram wisdom teaches that the root chakra, the muladhara, holds all the power in our journey towards realization and the journey through Consciousness after waking up. The root chakra holds the key to the inner journey, hence the importance of worshiping Lord Ganesh.

When we tread the Yogic path we realize the vastness of ourselves; we are like an onion, layered in realities, from the roots all the way to the crown – realities to unite with Source. Tantiram, the core of tantra, is the experience of orgasmic bliss within each and all layers of reality that we can enhance through our daily yoga. When we awaken to the wholeness of yoga, we transform our primal energies of sex, sensuality and survival instinct into evolved Angelic potent thoughts of manifestation. Our daily yoga is a tool to transforming and evolving through the embrace of wholeness, the tantiram. Most Hatha yoga teachings involve invoking the root chakra to awaken and work with Mother Kundalini. When we journey inward, we know Mother Kundalini as another state of Consciousness; through this awareness we ride through the inner fire, awakening each chakra. Each chakra holds the secrets of all layered realities, manifesting in Harmony, abundance and Divine grace.

This wholeness is the union with Source that holds the nature of bliss and the understanding of the 'I Am' experience, as in the bold statement, 'I Am God'. Lord Siva experienced is 'Satchidananda' – the experience of the 'Now' as bliss.

BE THE GURU: SECRETS WITHIN YOGA

– AWAKEN TO UNDERSTAND THE SELF AS CONSCIOUSNESS ITSELF, THE GURU.

Yoga works on the push and pull factor.

The push is our own daily discipline and effort. The pull is grace. This grace is attributed to our Guru whom we invoke through our daily yoga. In a yoga class, expressing reverence and gratitude to the yoga teacher at the beginning and end of each yoga session enhances the inherent goodness of the inner journey of yoga.

In nearly all Eastern philosophies, importance, reverence and respect is given to the Guru – the one who opens the door to our inner wisdom.

This Guru is most times a living master or it can sometimes be a spiritual being whose grace and guidance enhances our journey through Consciousness. Awareness from a Yogic perspective is the wisdom guiding us beyond the state of the 'no-thought' where the mind has no more thoughts. This 'awareness' as the wisdom behind thought is the Guru. In yoga, as we journey through Consciousness and states beyond the mind, the awareness beyond the mind as the Guru continues to guide us.

The mind is the tool to awareness and the journey beyond Consciousness. Breath is the key to utilizing the mind. Each thought carries energy, and thoughts of our Guru carry an expanded energy of wisdom that guides, transforms and evolves us. When we invoke our personal Guru/s to guide us through our Yogic journey, we are guided through a higher wisdom connection that is both fulfilling and nourishing.

The Guru Chakra

Guru Consciousness comes from awareness of the chakra which is located above the navel and known by the Yogis as the Guru Chakra (not described in any textbooks or intellectual teachings of yoga). Tapping into this energy field just above the navel, we possess vast unlimited energy even as we awaken to the primal wisdom of higher Consciousness. Yogis activate this energy field above the navel, the Guru Chakra, to climb above Consciousness that gives the freedom to be beyond hunger, heat/cold and sleep/tiredness.

With daily practice invoking our Gurus, we master Consciousness to become the Guru. Expanded Consciousness is Mother Kundalini. When we realize that the Guru is Kundalini and that Kundalini is a state of Consciousness, we are the Guru.

How to incorporate the Guru Chakra in your daily yoga practice: [It is recommended to practice the Sun Salutation sequence to incorporate the invoking of the Guru. The Sun Salutation is a sequence of postures that helps us warm up at the beginning stages of yoga. In this sequence, from posture to posture, awareness of breath, the mind and the body unites with ease.]

1. Invoke your Guru at the start of the sequence as you bring your palms together in Anjali mudra (palms together at the front of the chest). Remember your Guru through each following sequence and through each breath.

2. Stand with the legs slightly apart, imagining yourself as a pyramid. Feel the root chakra within yourself as the center of the pyramid. Experience yourself as stable and steady while aware of each breath.

3. Inhale all the way down from the root chakra. Let the breath fill up from the lower belly and upwards.

4. In the retention of breath, be conscious of the spot above the navel. Contract the spot above the navel.

5. In the exhale, elongate the breath as a slow exhale while being conscious of the navel chakra and the Guru within your breath.

6. Do the entire sequence of Sun Salutation being aware of each breath as the journey within the breath invoking the Guru.

7. Through each posture, feel the Guru Chakra so that all effort from the body in making the postures comes from the Guru Chakra.

8. Upon completing the Sun Salutation sequence, come back to the Anjali mudra (palms together at the front of the chest), exhale through the third eye, and visualize the Guru as Spirit within yourself.

Ultimately, through daily yoga, we realize our inner fire and the Gurus we have invoked as the higher Consciousness we awaken to be. The Guru within awakens as a blessing of yoga!

So be the Guru!

CONQUER TIME: EMPEROR EMPOWERMENT!

The difference between an emperor of time and a slave is that an emperor owns time and the realities within it, while a slave is trapped in seemingly uncontrollable natural ups and downs. Stepping into the Sabarmati Ashram of Mahatma Gandhi in Gujarat, India, it is mind-boggling to see that there are thousands of books written by one man and another few thousand books written about him.

This one man, Mahatma Gandhi, had far too many activities on his plate, apart from the already overwhelming initiatives he undertook in the freedom struggle of India. He did his fair share of chores for the upkeep of the Ashram. There was not a single piece of correspondence sent to him — from all parts of colonial India (that includes today's Pakistan and Bangladesh) and from all parts of the world — that was not answered by him personally. Added to all these daily activities was Gandhi's daily prioritization of time – to spin cotton for his own clothes, to garden, to tend his animals and meet the numerous people who showed up every day at his Ashram.

So how did Gandhi manage so much within 24 hours? What was his Yogic secret? Gandhi was named the 'Mahatma'— the 'Great Soul'— to denote the Yogi in him who was the emperor — the Yogi who had conquered time, reality and the limits of the human form.

In India, millions of gods and goddesses are worshiped in various forms. From the mystical Yogic perspective of the Siddhars, some of our most important visible forms of 'God' today are our wristwatches and our clocks. But when we learn how to align time with timelessness, we are in tune with the evolving grace that is the absolute gift of being born human.

Yes, everything comes back to time and how we are either enslaved within time, or timeless and free, when we can define time of our own accord, as an emperor.

Whether we like it or not, we are born into the 24-hour cycle of time, which is divided into day and night. We are born with a mind that is captured by limitations – limited by the number of hours we can spend in sleep, the number of hours we can be awake and the number of hours we can be in the dream state. This mind is also a slave to the past and its momentum. This can be attributed in part to 'karma', the law of equating the past within the present. This emotional roller-coaster creates lopsided realities and further traps the mind in seemingly uncontrollable natural ups and downs. As a slave, we then see our reality as if it were a movie, without any control over what unfolds, forgetting that it is a movie and we do have a choice.

We can of course choose to be a slave or an emperor!

An emperor owns time. So how do we begin setting ourselves free from time and redefining time and the realities unfolding before us? How do we become the emperor?

Light your Lamp at least once a day!

From beginning to end, life's journey is between us, as individuals, and Source/God. In between Source and our true identity as Soul is our mind. Lighting our outer and inner lamp is key to all meditation effort, as we are able to let go and surrender all our worries, emotions and good and bad thoughts to Source. We still the mind to a place of calm, Harmony and optimism.

When we light a lamp to connect with Source/our inner self/infinity once a day, we are lighting and manifesting the inner lamp within ourselves. Lighting our inner lamp at least once a day breaks our entrapment in the 24-hour cycle of time by awakening us to the space of timelessness, which we experience during these moments spent with ourselves and Source. The experience of connecting to Source is guided by joy, happiness and liberation each day, with our objective being to have more and more of this.

Once a week, set aside one day to take a supreme holiday.

Ultimately, if we can prioritize one day a week just for us to reconnect to Source, our journey to become the emperor has begun. This one special day is for us to meditate, pray, do yoga or anything that will bring us to our own centers. It is not about our creative zeal or even our family, let alone our career. It is about us expanding our Consciousness to be Source/infinite, devoid of our mind, reclaiming ourselves as Spirit having a human experience.

Once every fortnight, utilize the days of the full Moon and new Moon as vortices of time to penetrate beyond ordinary Consciousness.

The full Moon period is a vortex of time that enables us to make a shift in shaping our existing realities. The full Moon directly works with our minds. From the Yogic perspective, when we observe this full Moon vortex of time with a focus on Lord Vishnu, we are able to transform our spiritual and material realities through the mind and increase its ability to focus on expanding the realities we truly desire.

Likewise, during the new Moon, the vortex of being and Spirit, we are able to leapfrog our evolution as we observe the worship (Siva Linga Puja – described in its own section) of Lord Siva. In the space of infinity, where Consciousness is forever expanding, our mind and our realities can be taken several notches above. The Yogis prefer the new Moon vortex as it offers the chance to preset the mind to a much higher 'station' in its ever-expanding Consciousness, able to make each thought potent. Observe Mahasivratri as a Yogi — be Lord Siva!

The grandest and the most powerful vortex of time/timelessness is the once-a-year enlightening vortex of time: Mahasivratri, the supreme night of the Yogi, Lord Siva. This vortex, based on the lunar calendar, has been observed by hundreds of millions of regular householders and spiritual seekers dating far back through the history of India. Observe this potent vortex of time and start your Yogic inner journey by way of fasting, meditating, pilgrimage, silence and worship at least two weeks before this sacred day.

Slowly but surely, we begin to realize that we can slip out of the limitations of time (as we do in sleep) and the limitations of the mind, to attain the Yogic Turiya state — 'sleepless sleep'. As Mahasivratri nears, through the grace of this enlightening vortex of time and our own effort, we easily step into the state of Turiya — we experience Spirit having a human experience. On the night of Mahasivratri, most spiritual warriors try not to sleep, in order to get the blessings of this sacred night. We Yogis are already in the beautiful sleepless sleep state of Turiya, a state of inspired awareness, and on this night, we become the vast infinity of being, Lord Siva. Each of us has our own unique experience of 'being God'.

After having the sacred, fruitful experience of being Lord Siva on Mahasivratri, the mind will never be the same. Realities naturally align themselves to Harmony. Innermost desires and highest purposes are fulfilled through the empowered super-mind that has experienced being God — the enlightened mind.

Once a week-— one day every week – we recapture and deepen our Mahasivratri experience through the inner journey we undertake. It is a supreme holiday we can give ourselves to renew our Source connection

Every day, when we light our lamp, we carry forward our expanding Consciousness to even vaster realms while we are in the state of super-Consciousness — the state of Turiya. Our every thought now comes from the genius of the mind that is aligned to its pristine Source state. Ultimately, we understand and awaken to the need to be in a perpetual state of joy, bliss and inspiration, and we set our daily discipline to attain this Angelic state of being.

All this discipline of being united with Source leads us to be in the magic of the 'Now' moment. Being in the 'Now' as Spirit having a human experience, the karma that limits us is transmuted to become opportunities for growth. Where is the past momentum of karma if we are no longer in the past or future, but in the now, not as humans, but as Spirit having a human experience? In this enlightened state, where each thought is empowerment to further embrace reality, free of karmic restraints — we are the emperor.

The secret behind the dazzling work and life mesSage left behind by Mahatma Gandhi, in his books and in his legacy, can be attributed to the state of Turiya he was in. Every day, he was up by 3 a.m., ready to start the day in communal prayers. He seldom took a nap during the day. He held another communal prayer meeting at 10 pm, after which he would read before going to sleep. Being in the state of Turiya, he was a cause of setting into humanity's Consciousness the reality of Harmony, love and Peace. Mahatma Gandhi was an emperor, a 'Maharaj,' who conquered time as a Yogi.

When humanity sets itself free by awakening to timelessness, we will chart the destiny for our future, through a Consciousness where physical and material abundance flows naturally, in Harmony and fulfillment for all. Peace reigns supreme where Consciousness is.

BLESSINGS THROUGH RESONANCE: MANTRA POWER

The most potent blessing we could ever receive from a Sage, Yogi or any Enlightened Master is to receive the uplifting, igniting grace of our own Consciousness. In the ancient pre-vedic Tamil language, the word mantra is mentioned as 'mandiram' which also means magic – the ability to transform reality in a moment. Called 'deeksha', which means initiation, the giving of a mantra by the Guru to the initiate is the single most important ritual, as the mantra serves the initiate's lifelong spiritual journey through the thread of ancient resonance.

Traditionally in India, conveying awakening Consciousness is done especially through mantra. In the mystical Yogic tradition of the South Indian Siddhars, there is less emphasis on written or oral teachings; much of the wisdom is conveyed through the mantra energy that awakens the inner knowledge.

Mantra recitation can be said to be the mother of meditation. With the recitation of a mantra, the mind immediately focuses on a single thought, leading to transcendence – awareness beyond the mind. By reciting the mantra, effortlessness in meditation is enhanced even while doing mundane chores.

When we meet a higher conscious being in the form of a saint, Yogi, or even disguised in the ordinary, as a taxi driver, we know that we are uplifted by the words, action or simply the mere presence of that person. Higher conscious beings flow with a vibration of Peace and Harmony. It is said that when Buddha walked from place to place, crisscrossing each village and town, his presence was felt by people over 10 miles away. On feeling his presence as Peace, love and calm, thousands would gather near Buddha to experience more of this vibrancy.

There are many scientific studies on meditation that have proven that meditation gives more benefits to society than merely inner Peace for the meditator. The effect of mass meditation has been noted to affect surrounding areas by creating a significant drop in the crime rate. For example, when the founder of Transcendental Meditation, Maharishi Mahesh Yogi, conducted a group meditation with hundreds of people, a drop in crime rates in the surrounding area was observed to be consistent. This energy field produced by meditation has, for a long time, been referred to by Yogis as Consciousness.

The secrets of power within mantras are:

1. Mantras serve as a bridge of Consciousness:
When receiving the mantra from a Guru, understand its significance: this is an initiation in which we are forever connected in Consciousness with the Guru. By reciting the mantra, the seeker is able to climb above states of Consciousness and become the master. Every time we chant our mantra, we are invoking the presence of our Guru. An enlightened master's presence in our lives is protecting, nurturing and guiding us, until gradually, our own Consciousness becomes the presence of the master.

2. Mantra chants create the specific realities we desire:
Each mantra holds a specific dimension of reality. For example, when we chant a mantra for the Goddess of abundance, we will see that we reflect abundance in our realities. Understand the power of recitation of mantras to be tapping into the realities we desire. For instance, when there is a deep fear and we recite a specific mantra, we are creating an energy field to protect ourselves. The more we trust the abilities of the mantra and recite the mantra from our heart in its intent, the better the mantra works to create the specific reality that we seek.

3. Mantras shift and transform our thoughts and thinking patterns:

Through chanting the mantra, we begin to tune into the inherent vibrations within the mantra and come into alignment with those higher vibrations. When we do this, our mind also perceives thoughts from a higher place.

4. Mantras are a manifestation tool:
When we chant the mantra, our mind is slowly brought to a singular focus – like a magnifying glass that converts sunlight into fire. Any intent held through the mantra is magnified due to the intensity of focus and an intent that has been held long is thus brought to reality.

5. Mantras are supreme prayers:
Nearly all mantras carry the intent of invoking a specific facet of God/Source. Through chanting the mantra we develop a singular focus on the invoked Deity. Extended over years of chanting, we realize our connection to the invoked Source/God more and more, and with greater ease.

6. Mantras fine-tune our breath and optimal thinking process:
By chanting the mantra, our inner journey to Source/God has begun. Slowly we begin to realize our breath is becoming deeper and slower, thereby utilizing more of our lungs. This is a natural process that reciting a mantra accomplishes. With enhanced breathing, our mind also thinks optimally from the center of Harmony.

7. Reciting the mantra awakens the state of bliss:
As we chant the mantra, we transcend the limits of the mind. Reciting mantras induces bliss due to the mind slipping away from its past momentum and acquiring the stress free 'Now' moment. We awaken to the 'Now' moment that is devoid of worry about the past or future when the mind is subdued to the ever-present Harmony in the core of our being. We are able to experience a state of joy within the mantra that the Sages of antiquity held on to. Holding on to this state of joy embedded within the mantra, we begin to expand this state of

joy in our being – as in a body of bliss, as in realities of bliss and in perceiving all realities from the state of bliss.

8. The power and potency within the mantra can constantly be increased:
We realize the mantra by chanting it, as a way of connecting our Consciousness with our Guru, who gave the mantra to us. When we perform acts of goodness and kindness (dharma) we are increasing the power within the mantra. The mantra serves as the facilitator to higher Consciousness and when we utilize the wisdom of Higher Consciousness to do good, we are allowing the flow of grace that is awakened through our expanding Consciousness.

9. Mantras are empowered with the 'cooking' process:
The more we chant the mantra, the more potent and powerful the mantra becomes. As we chant the mantra over longer periods of time and over the years, we realize the mantra's effect on reality in daily miracles and its potency in realities created. With time, the mantras we recite mature and get 'cooked'. When the mantra is 'cooked' for a period of time, it can then be given to another as a field of Consciousness that easily lights up anyone ready for more Consciousness. Even to simply listen to the mantra chant of an enlightened master can shift our Consciousness, partly because the mantra has been 'cooked' by the master, and partly because the mantra is embedded with the blessings of all masters who have chanted the mantra before – the lineage behind the mantra.

10. Chant the mantra and awaken to all the goodness of higher Consciousness:
Chanting the mantra transforms the mind to an effortless meditative state. When the mind is in a meditative state, our Consciousness expands to imbibe all positive attributes – such as less stress, increased empathy, more focus, more optimism, more unconditional love and so on.

11. Mantras carry the vibratory presence of our Guru and all the preceding Gurus as the lineage Presence:
It is wise to receive a mantra from an Enlightened Master, as most mantras are passed on from Guru to disciple; the mantra will have been chanted by each Guru over an entire life time. When we chant the mantra, we are tapping into the primal vibrations of all masters of the past and bringing this energy into our own expanding Consciousness. When we recite mantras that have a strong lineage, we are able to align to this ancient lineage of the Gurus, manifesting as guidance, protection and grace in our inner journey.

12. Chanting mantras is an optimal solution for those with Attention Deficit Disorder (ADD):
Recent scientific studies attest that meditation does help those with ADD. From childhood our mind seeks input from music, television or other data Sources. We have access to massive amounts of information through the world wide web, so it is only natural that our mind is trained to have an attention deficit. For these people, the form of meditation based on breath awareness and eradication of thoughts simply does not work, especially for those of us in urban areas. Reciting the mantra is perhaps the surest way to not only quieting the mind but also to train the mind to focus on a single point for a longer period of time.

13. Awaken the genius within:
Through chanting we enhance the mind's ability to meditate, to climb above the normal patterns of the mind. In 'climbing above the mind' we are able to think outside the box of limitations. Most of the amazing minds of history, such as Albert Einstein and Isaac Newton, were able to connect with the spiritual essence beyond the mind and 'see' the higher perspective that we refer to as 'genius' and great intelligence. When we go behind to understand the awareness that exists beyond our thought patterns and thinking processes, we are tapping into a state of super-Consciousness. This is what the Yogi Sages call the state of Turiya. Chanting leads us to this

super-Consciousness state that all beings of higher Consciousness experience.

14. Empower the mantra by constantly doing Dharma (heart's work):
The essence of the mantra is the energy field created between our own Consciousness and the Consciousness of the guru behind the mantra, therefore each act of goodness that we perform empowers the mantra in its potency. When we do charitable deeds, the mantra within us feeds on the good energies created to become even more potent.

15. Mantras enable the transformational journey within:
Through mantras we change the patterns of our past thinking. The spiritual history of India is filled with ignorant persons who used to be robbers and murderers. Wanting to change their lives, they began by surrendering to a mantra and then emerging as enlightened masters! All it takes to awaken the highest wisdom within ourselves is the initiation through mantra. Then our journey to become a master unfolds. When we are ready, the right mantra is received.

TURIYA STATE OF SUPER CONSCIOUSNESS

– AS REFLECTED BY RAMANA MAHARISHI AND MAHATMA GANDHI

When our meditation practice becomes true to ourselves and states of joy alight, we are in the state of Turiya. Turiya is higher Consciousness, what the Sages call the sleepless sleep. Turiya is the experience of the liberated. The liberated are the Self-realized.

Sri Ramana Maharshi, one of Mother India's enlightened masters, would awaken the Turiya state of higher Consciousness of any seeker who sought his blessings simply through silent presence. His simple gaze would awaken a seeker to realization.

This enlightened Sage would explain complex Yogic terminologies through simple stories and often in just a few words, leaving the truth of understanding to be realized through the experience of the seeker.

He would illustrate the state of Turiya through this story:
'Once upon a time, three thieves ruled over a jungle. If anyone entered this jungle, they never could escape these thieves. The first thief was violent, merciless, cruel and lazy. The second thief always wanted things done and was constantly in action, running around the forest, checking out the neighboring towns, never at one place for very long. The third thief however had goodness in him. He was Peaceful and happy but sworn into the company of the other two thieves since they were living together in the forest as a family.

'One day, Manidan had to go through the forest. As soon as he entered the forest, he was captured by the three thieves, who tied him up. Imprisoned, Manidan prayed to Source for freedom from this harassment and cruelty, not knowing any other relief. Hearing the prayers, the third thief, the good one, came to his rescue. While the first thief, the bad one, was sleeping, and the second thief was as usual doing his rounds, the good thief released Manidan from his bonds. The good thief took Manidan to the outer boundaries of the forest and said, 'Walk out to your freedom beyond the entrapment of this forest and the robbers who dwell in it. From now on, remember that you are not Manidan anymore. You are a Deva, an Angel.' Manidan walked out to his true reality, with the name and identity of Deva.'

'The Thieves' represent the three states of mind. The first state of mind is Tamas – the lower state of the mind that is ignorant. The tamas state is characterized as the nature of sloth, anger, violence and all the lower tendencies of human beings. The second state of mind is Rajas, which describes a person who is active and action-oriented, liked those who live in fast-paced societies of the West, or as city dwellers – those who live in survival mode. The third state of mind, called Satva, is characterized as the Peaceful, tranquil nature that knows basic goodness in each pure thought.

Any time we pray, meditate, or contemplate Source, our satvic mind steps in to untie us from the unique bond of ego and the mental patterns we experience in human limitation. The 'forest' is the human mind that we enter into through this birth. 'Manidan', the man captured and confined in the mind forest, is the humanness of ourselves – Manidan in Tamil means 'the human'. And 'Deva' is the Being that arises from within when we are shown freedom by the third state of the mind, the Satvic nature within ourselves. 'Deva' in both Tamil and Sanskrit means 'the Angel'.

This Deva state is Turiya – the spirit having a human experience as a higher conscious being. In the state of Turiya – experienced as expanded realities – we are able to tap into our potential of genius wherever we choose to focus our attention.

The Turiya state is a common denominator of inspiration for all people. For instance, an artist while painting, a mother suckling her baby, or anyone who is aligned to the genius of perfection, steps into Turiya states, where the doer forgets time, hunger and tiredness in the intensity of inspiration. Every higher conscious master imparts wisdom through the alignment of being in states of Turiya through prayer, contemplation, meditation and inspiration.

The majority of humanity experiences Turiya unconsciously in states of joy. In this fleeting flash of a moment, joy reveals itself and sets the person in pursuit of more of this joy.

A Yogi consciously seeks the state of joy within until the state of Turiya begins to be his or her perpetual meditation mode – of being in love, as love, in every moment. Disciplines form around the desire to have more joy, leading us to do our daily yoga, lighting a lamp to Source. All of this leads to a mind that is in the joy of awareness, mindfulness and bliss, which is the nature of the Turiya state.

Those liberated and blessed by Turiya are Mahatmas – the immense awakened souls such as Mahatma Gandhi. If you are traveling through Mother India, visit Sabarmati Ashram, in Gujarat. Here Gandhi's Divine presence is enshrined in the form of the many books he wrote and the innumerable articles, notes and books written about him.

Gandhi was definitely blessed in the state of Turiya, demonstrated in his need for little sleep (less than four hours each day) and going to bed and waking up with prayer and chanting. He loved reading and would fall asleep by midnight and had no need to nap during the day; occasionally he would cat nap for less than 30 minutes. Gandhi said, 'If you are really tired during the day, meditate twice as much, to wipe tiredness away.'

In 'Prayer', Gandhi's most personal book, he reveals the Turiya state. In this autobiographical book, this great leader of humanity discloses a rare portrait of himself – more open and frank in discussing his intimate spiritual life. In understanding and celebrating each breath in tune with Source, Gandhi describes being in a meditative state throughout his daily work, and how intensely inspired each moment was, even during difficult times. He reports going to sleep, with his final plunge into the depth of sleep through prayer, and then waking up each morning with prayer; through this practice, he attained the higher conscious mind that could manifest magnificent realities as a Mahatma.

A historically significant incident was recorded by the disciples of Sri Ramana Maharshi, when that Saint was asked what he thought about Gandhi. (This was at a time when the title of 'Mahatma' was not yet conferred on Gandhi, about 20 years before India won independence and when the freedom struggle of India against the British imperialism had waned.) At that time, Gandhi was in a political wilderness, with no breakthrough with the British likely in the struggle for freedom. Sri Ramana Maharishi responded with total confidence: 'Gandhi operates from the Aadi Atma Shakti, and no matter what, he will accomplish the objective of the freedom struggle.'

Sri Ramana Maharshi meant that Gandhi had tapped into the powerful 'Soul Force', the primal energy of the soul, and this awakened Turiya state would lead him to victory. Sri Ramana Maharshi recognized the Turiya state in Gandhi, years before Gandhi was truly acknowledged by all of India for winning independence.

Attain the Turiya state through your daily practice to celebrate your union with Source. By cultivating this daily practice, Consciousness is expanded, making each thought potent and able to manifest the most harmonious, abundant and inspired realities! Imagine the power of a million Mahatmas shaping our global realities as blessings of Turiya for all of humanity! Through Turiya be a Mahatma.

MAHASIVRATRI: THE NIGHT OF THE YOGI/YOGINI

– TIME VORTEX OF ENLIGHTENMENT

Once a year, a powerful time vortex presents itself, whereby we can attain enlightenment with ease. This is the day/night of Mahasivratri. For a Yogi/Yogini, Mahasivratri is the 'Day/Night of Yoga', the time to transcend, transform, evolve and attain liberation. Mahasivratri has been observed as the single most important vortex of time by both Yogis and householders in India for thousands of years. Based on the planetary alignment with Earth and the lunar cycle, this vortex of time holds the objectives of yoga – Spirit having a human experience; liberation from the limits of the mind; and having the grace of Source in our daily realities.

In practical realities, Mahasivratri offers:

- An ideal time to detox the body
- The time to detox the mind – letting go of the past and karmic imprints of limitations
- An ideal time to create an intent of resolution and a supreme prayer
- An inspiration to awaken the Yogi within
- A potent time to break free from the stagnancy of life to enable us to more easily evolve into a life more attuned to our higher purpose
- To awaken to the joyfulness of 'Being' a person of higher Consciousness and thereby imbibing all the qualities of higher Consciousness: abundance, Harmony, love and wisdom.

In the Western world it is truly beautiful to witness the growth of yoga as a practice, as an exercise and as a lifestyle itself. A drop of honey will lead to the honey pot. Practicing yoga naturally provides benefits of health and less stress, but beyond it all is the experience of gravitating towards Source, expressed in words such as 'freedom', 'oneness', 'bliss', 'inspired', 'in the Now', and so on. When we go deeper into the science of yoga to understand yoga as a journey through Consciousness, we realize that words such as 'liberation'' and 'enlightenment' are not distant concepts but an amazing experience we can have in our daily realities. Observing Mahasivratri does ease us into awakening the potential underlying objectives within yoga.

The worship of Lord Siva (known as Lord Shiva in Northern India) is essentially advaita, which means: awakening to the Oneness of Source in who we are and in everything we perceive. 'Si' is the Spirit that we are; 'Va' is the Goddess, that of experience. Siva is the awakening experience to be the vast void that holds all the universes. This awakening is related to the experience of being the Spirit – the vast Soul that is beyond our 'I' identification, Siva. This is the root understanding to Lord Siva, the male and female within each of us. Likewise, 'Yogi' refers also to the feminine counterpart 'Yogini'.

In the spiritual depth of India, most Yogis who undergo deep tapas (meditative penance) seldom coming out for months at a time, take a break from their meditative state on this one day. These Sages come out to bless humanity during this period of Mahasivratri. For one on the path of yoga, this is the night to experience and actually be the Eternal Yogi.

This day of Mahasivratri is based on the lunar calendar; during this period our Consciousness easily condenses into Divine awareness. From the Yogic perspective, the Moon directly influences the mind and our Consciousness. Each month, the new Moon and full Moon energies offer their own unique power as the Earth rotates around the Sun in its oval-shaped orbit through the year. Each day of the Moon cycle holds a specific nature and in the mystical traditions of yoga, each day is attributed to a specific Goddess; each Goddess holds a unique facet of energy based on the Moon phase. Each full Moon and new Moon period holds a specific vortex of energy. New Moons hold the Consciousness of Lord Siva, the Spirit experience, while full Moons hold the awareness and the mind, the energies of Lord Vishnu. Every month, there is one Sivaratri – a potent time to meditate and worship deeply, and once a year, the grand Mahasivratri (maha means great) near the new Moon period.

Mahasivratri and Turiya: One of the key observances during the night of Mahasivratri is to stay awake all night. In reality, it is not about being a weekend warrior staying up all night singing, chanting and dancing, but about training ourselves to go beyond the mind and its sleep pattern through meditative practice. At the time vortex of Mahasivratri, we are able to experience the 'sleepless sleep' state with less effort.

The many objectives of yoga from the original intent of the Sages unravel with the experience of Turiya and the grace of Mahasivratri.

- When we unite the limited mind with Source, we 'yoke' the unlimited potential to expand human realities to its mastery, as an artist does while painting.
- When we realize that we are the Infinite Spirit dwelling in the body as the 'I Am' experience, we are able to attain the highest perspective of realities that surround us and attain the radiance of blissful being.
- Upon realizing that our body is a shrine that houses our Soul, well-being as good health flows naturally with us.
- Upon climbing above the mind as Spirit having a human experience, we realize the oneness of humanity, oneness of all life, and ourselves as the Oneness that is many. We awaken to the potent Angelic nature of realization to be compassionate.

- We are blessed with the attainment of higher Consciousness that is causal in abundance, as well as love, inspiration and fulfillment to all our aspirations.
- We awaken to the wisdom of karma, dharma and our highest purpose on planet Earth. We become the Angelic beings recreating heaven here on Earth.
- When we utilize yoga as a tool to Consciousness, we realize that the journey is beyond the mind and the natural states of sleep, being awake and dreaming.

Any higher conscious master of any culture or religion has the ability to bless reality through words and intent. This is because they are in touch with the higher conscious mind that is in union with Source, the mind state of Turiya. In deeper meditation, as we journey through the states of being awake, dreaming and sleeping, we realize each facet of the mind in levels of Consciousness. The Yogis dive beneath these layers to go beyond the mind, the thought patterns and karmic imprints, to the state of Turiya, the state of sleepless sleep. In the state of Turiya, the Yogis climb into timelessness to intensify the 'I Am' experience. In Mahasivratri, the key to celebrating Lord Siva is by staying awake all night long to experience the Yogic state of the mind, the Turiya. This higher conscious state of Turiya is the hidden experience that we are to be blessed with during Mahasivratri when staying awake through the night singing, meditating or/and chanting.

For more information and guidance please visit www.worldYogiday.org

LINGAM PUJA: MULTIPLY CONSCIOUSNESS

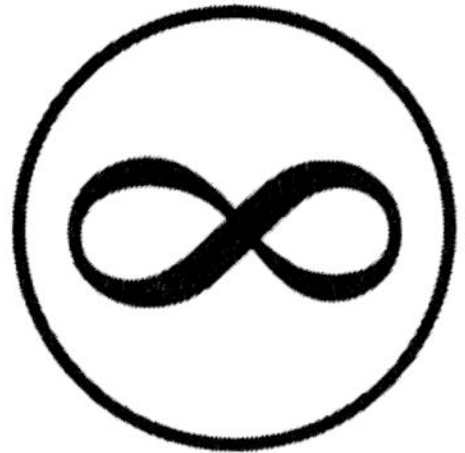

The Lingam Worship:

The worship of Lord Siva, represented in the form of a Lingam is the Siva Linga Puja. The Siva Lingam puja is the most personal and intimate time for a Yogi as it represents moments of absorption into the Divine, fully aware and intensely in union with Source through breath and as breathless joys. The discipline of doing the Siva Linga puja is considered the most potent of all Yogic practices. A is able to push through states of Consciousness and through grace, evolve to be the object of worship, to be Lord Siva – as in the journey into One to be Oneness.

In the Yogic traditions of mystical India, each precious moment as a human is for the purpose of enhancing more of Consciousness and coming closer to Source. This journey beyond Consciousness is heightened each day with deeper and even more empowerment in the awakened inner wisdom. After having woken up to be the Spirit, the Yogi then starts enhancing this experience through intensifying the bliss state. In this journey through Consciousness guided by bliss, the Yogi understands effort and progress as a Yogi through the push factor of one's own effort, and Divine grace as the pull factor – through the Siva Lingam puja.

What is a Puja?

A puja is not meditation, because a puja requires a highly alert and involved state of mind. During a puja, Source, or an object of worship, is celebrated in the physical form with offerings of flowers, milk, water and so on, along with mantra. A puja is a concentrated, enhanced form of worship and can be called the mother of all meditations – a puja leads to a mind that is meditative, the natural state of the mind that is defined as meditation. By doing a Siva Linga Puja, the Yogi is aligned to receive grace by invoking the power of the infinite Source for the self, and for the entire world.

Siva Linga Puja is performed by utilizing the Lingam as a representation of the infinite, and with the mind in a super aware state, connecting to Divine and the object of focus through offerings of the heart.

So, what is the meaning of the Lingam?
To Yogis, the Lingam is the most apt form representing the Infinite, as the form of stambha – the beginning-less and endless pillar. The traditional description of the Lingam representing the phallus is only part of the meaning behind the Lingam. Yes, the Lingam is the representation of the 'Wand of Light' as the experience of our own inner Light rushing above through the spine.

When a Yogi performs the Lingam Puja, he or she is invoking the union of the infinite Spirit from within and the Infinite God Almighty of formlessness, to be the dweller in the Lingam, the form. The Lingam serves to house, represent and radiant the energies of Infinity. Later through history, by way of Western historians and through ways of convenience in hypothesis, a Lingam began being pegged to the meaning of phallus because of its shape.

How is a Siva Linga Puja performed?
- Attain or purchase a small Siva Lingam. You will need a few utensils that will help contain the water, milk and other offerings you may pour over the Lingam.
- Attain, receive or learn simple mantras, preferably for Ganesh, Lord Siva and Goddess Sakti. Your Siva Linga Puja is an inner journey through mantras, a journey of uniting your external realities and infinite inner realities through the puja. You use the mind in focus and surrender all thoughts through the fire of bhakti, devotional love. Once a day or once a week or whenever convenient, commit to doing a Siva Linga Puja.

The Inner Journey of the Siva Lingam Puja:
Prepare Yourself:
Prepare yourself for the Siva Linga Puja as a very personal journey between you and Source. Having a shower or washing your face helps to refresh your mind and body. Set aside at least 45 minutes of uninterrupted time. Create a sacred space for yourself, preferably an altar space that can hold and carry forward positive energies of a Siva Linga Puja. Gather offerings of flowers, water, milk or anything else you may feel like offering to the Lingam.

Abishekam:
An abisheka is a religious bathing ceremony that is usually done with sacred water. There is no right or wrong way in doing the abishekam. Begin by first reciting the mantra, invoking Lord Siva. Connect your breath to the mantra resonance and feel the invoked 'Presence' through your chanting. Now slowly begin pouring water or milk over the Lingam, invoking the Divine Infinite in the Lingam. (The milk may be used later as Prasad, Divine sanctified offerings.) After the Lingam has been bathed and cleansed, it is ready for the Puja.

Siva Lingam Puja:
Have many flowers or many petals of flowers that you will offer the Lingam with every mantra recited, invoking Lord

Siva. Ideally, when Lord Siva is invoked, it is perfect wisdom to invoke the Divine Goddess to complete the wholeness of the Divine. We end this puja invoking the awakened mind state, the God of sustenance and abundance, Lord Vishnu.

Invoke Blessings of Source:
A Siva Lingam Puja is powerful, as we have invoked the power of Infinity in our realities. As we bring the Siva Lingam Puja to closure, from the depth of depth, invoke Peace through reciting 'Shanthi'. By expanding to the infinite vastness we are bringing forth blessings of Peace into our own human form and realities. Create an intent in 'Peace' i.e., may this Peace be for all the living or; may this Peace be for my own health and the health of all of humanity. Blessed are the messengers and custodians of Peace.

Sacred Shrine/Altar at your Heart Shrine:
After a Siva Lingam Puja, store the Lingam at an altar space to keep the Divine energies and blessings vibrant in our physical and spiritual realities.

Benefits of a Siva Lingam Puja:

1. Grace to be a Yogi: When we surrender our total focus of the mind to Source, through the puja, the mind develops the ability to rejoice in the dance of stillness. This dance of stillness is the Mother of all meditative practices.
2. Evolve and Be God: As we invoke the presence of Source, holding the focus through our mantras, we are drawing more and more proximity to the object of worship and gradually, we attain all the attributes we are invoking, i.e., we slowly evolve to be Angelic, invoking the presence of God/Source.
3. Awaken our innate genius: We awaken to the deeper dimensions of Consciousness within us that triggers the innate special powers within ourselves, the 'Siddhis'. The Siddhis are the unique special abilities awakened in each of us, such as musical genius, the ability to see the future, the awakening of various extra sensory perceptions, etc. Yogis tend to disregard this awakening of various facets of the mind as it distracts us from the power of worship that grows in potency through humility.
4. Soul Empowerment: We wake up to the joys and bliss of experiencing Source/God- 'Ananda'. This joy ebbing from the bottom of the heart through our Lingam Puja is a higher conscious vibratory state. To be in this bliss form state is to be God – with Lord Siva described as Satchidananda, the bliss form. Slowly but surely, our realities too begin to vibrate at the higher frequencies of this Divine bliss.
5. Deepen our yoga practice: After having done the Siva Lingam puja, we understand the deeper journey within our daily yoga practice through the various sequences. In fact, it is advisable to do the Siva Lingam Puja after doing our Hatha yoga practice in order to seat the enormous vast immense energies of Source within us through the awakened nerve

centers, the nadis. Hatha yoga and the Siva Lingam Puja are naturally compatible and enhancing for each other.

6. Live the Magic of Now: To experience being God/Source; worship the Infinite Almighty through the mind and breath; attain grace of inner wisdom as a journey through Consciousness – this makes us Angelic and God-like. Slowly but surely, we not only awaken to the vastness we each truly are, but are also guided, protected and gifted with the most valuable gift of this human birth – to be able to celebrate the 'Now' moment completely.
7. Multiply Potency of Consciousness: Worshipping the Lingam is multiplying Consciousness. As we invoke ourselves to be Spirit, the Holy Ghost, we celebrate Lord Almighty Source of Infinite as in Form, empowering this Form to be Formlessness ever more.
8. Be Blessed: Lord Siva, the nameless Infinite Being invoked represents blessings of wellbeing, wisdom and highest purpose as the Yogi.

GRACE OF FOOD: SIDDHAR WISDOM

Food determines our wellbeing. Food is also medicine in its ability to heal and immunize. As a vital input into ourselves, food also determines our thinking and thought patterns. Food is energy. We enhance the energy of the food we eat through gratitude, reverence and invoking the Divine. There are of course, countless ways to say grace before eating our food as each culture, religion and families have different ways to express gratitude. From the Siddhar perspective, food also has a component of dharma, basic goodness, as an energy field to be enhanced.

In India, it is a normal cultural practice to offer food to guest before eating, even if the guests are strangers. This practice of offering food has deep meaning at a dharmic level. Nearly every saint, sadhu, guru and Yogi in India would agree that offering food as dharma to feed others is the most potent of all actions – simply because, as Siddhar Rajaswamy says, 'The stomach pit is the only pit in the human body that can be satisfied, and every human, rich or poor, goes through the pangs of hunger. Food also represents the body and when we feed people, we set into motion the grace of well-being, not only for ourselves but for humanity itself.'

Let us begin with this story to understand how we may say grace before eating. The story is from the time of the Mahabharata, when the Pandavas, the five brothers (the good guys) are in exile, hiding in the forest. The Pandavas were married to Draupadi, a Goddess incarnate who was graced with Lord Krishna in the Divine relationship of a brother.

The Kauravas, the hundred cousins (the bad guys) discovered their cousins, the Pandavas' hiding place in the forest

Determined to inflict damage on the Pandavas, the Kauravas summoned Sage Durvasa. Sage Durvasa had undertaken tremendous tapas (deep meditation) and due to the potency of his tapas, every word he spoke came true. But Sage Durvasa had a vice – in spite of years of intense penance that gave him enormous siddhis (powers), he had not conquered anger. Durvasa was extremely short tempered and in a moment, he could curse anyone.

The Kauravas requested Durvasa to go and visit the Pandavas in the forest, intending that Durvasa would arrive at the little hut dwelling of the Pandavas just after they had eaten their food. Durvasa and his retinue of disciples arrived at the Pandava brothers' house and Draupadi was shocked and worried. She realized that there was absolutely no food left in the house.

As she stood in silence, Durvasa muttered, 'Divine Host, my disciples and I are hungry and tired. We will go and take a bath in the nearby stream and we will come back to your home shortly.' Draupadi understood this to mean that Durvasa and his disciples needed to be fed and they would be taking a bath to give Draupadi time to cook their food!

As Durvasa and his entourage left to have a bath, Draupadi started crying out to Lord Krishna, 'Please come and save me Krishna!' Lord Krishna appeared and asked Draupadi why she should panic when there was already all the food of the universe available to her. Draupadi replied, 'Krishna, this is not a joke. Don't you realize that we have no food in this household? Every morsel of food has been consumed.' Lord Krishna put his hand into the pot in which the food was cooked, picking up a tiny morsel of leftover rice. He put this in His mouth saying, 'May all the stomachs of all living beings be full and satisfied!'

Meanwhile, Durvasa and his disciples had just completed bathing and were returning in anticipation to eat the food they thought was being prepared by Draupadi. Just then, their stomachs felt full! As a follower of the Indian custom of eating well as a guest, in order to honor the host, Durvasa was now perplexed. How could he face Draupadi if he could not eat well? Unable to meet this obligation, Durvasa and his retinue quietly slipped away.

This story expresses Siddhar wisdom. Whenever we prepare to eat, if we could for a moment close our eyes, imagine ourselves to be the vast Spirit, like Lord Krishna, and make a deep wishful intent: 'May all creatures and may all of humanity be fed'. Then, as an ethereal Being, if we inhale the food's aroma and say gratitude to Source for having given us this food, we set into momentum potent dharma. The very thought and intent to feed all others before we eat is blessings of grace in our lives and to bless the food before us.

'Great indeed is the power acquired through austerity to endure hunger. But greater still is the power of those who relieve the hunger of others.'
-Tirukkural 23:225, Spiritual Poetry of a Tamil Saint, Siddhar Thiruvalluvar

When we understand the significance of imagining and creating an intent to feed every stomach on planet Earth before consuming our own food, even if we are physically not doing so, we are reflecting a positive thought of vibrational energy. When we acknowledge ourselves to be the Universal Spirit and intend the fulfillment of every hunger, we invoke the energy of the Source, to enable this. Accompanied by gratitude as our reality in the moment, the food becomes cleansed, energized and serves our well-being.

The Genius of Consciousness

The innate genius now awakens as we become savants.

Various studies on savants show the correlation of the left brain with the right brain that attributes this genius.
The 'awakened' conceptualize the vastness of spiritual beingness or connectivity to the infinite with the practical facets of thinking from the inspired flow that enables them to excel in what they do.

While Albert Einstein considered one of the foremost geniuses of the 20th century, has transformed scientists' understanding of physics and astronomy with his theories, the intellect of Einstein himself has remained misunderstood.

Ever since pathologist, Dr. Thomas Harvey harvested the scientist's brain in 1955, researchers have tried to crack the mystery of Einstein's genius by observing that brain.
A new study, published in the journal, Brain, on September 24, 2013, suggests that the two hemispheres in Einstein's brain were unusually well connected.

All scientists of ancient India's past were Yogis—awake and liberated beings who could think outside the box of the mind. Spirituality's offspring is Consciousness that adheres and creates newer frontiers for humanity as in intellect and realities.

In the Yogic philosophy is the chakra system wherein, the crown chakra, when awake, is called the sahasrara (thousand petals of the lotus awake). Once awake, the petals, as awareness, forever stands awake. This awakening experience is like stepping out of one level of Consciousness to another higher level while understanding the concept of freedom as being liberated from the mind as in its limits and past momentum of thoughts.

When we have a near death experience or a powerful experience of awakening, we have, ourselves, lifted beyond the limits of the mind and forever, the way we think and perceive our realities have changed. In this state, is the purest state of joy ever experienced and there is no reason (or all the reasons) that is behind this state of joy.

This experience has been expressed by Sages of all cultures and religions throughout the world. The Yogis of the eastern traditions describe this as the lotus having blossomed with the joy states mentioned as bliss. The Yogis attribute the state of bliss as in being Lord Siva, the form of bliss. This is, in reality, the depiction of all religions, the Spirit having the human experience.

Almost immediately after this spiritual experience, the pursuit into even deeper thresholds of seeking for more of this joyfulness begins. This seeking can be described as God, Infinity, Source, Supreme-Self and all other characterizations. Some are born with this awareness while others are activated into this awareness at some point in their life. The moment such awareness is activated, most persons plunge deeper into uncovering the states of joy.
While a few of those who have experienced this first awakening take to a lifelong meditative effort, as the monks and Yogis, some return back to the normal realities of the society as in marrying, having children and running a household, having a career and holding responsibilities.

In the mystical path of the Siddhars, returning back to the society to serve humanity from the highest Consciousness has been indicated to be the fastest way to evolve.

When awake and in the society's structures of responsibility, there is a different perception to how we spend each of our moments, our definition of time, our way of perceiving what success is and our ability to understand life at its best and worst situations. All this, as in thinking from a higher place of

Consciousness and then relating to the mundane realities faced, is the linking of the left brain and the right brain.

As in physical exercise, where the muscle gets stronger with each day, this exercise is the mental exercise of relating the left brain and the right brain.

These are important teachings of the Sages to exercise the left brain and the right brain and in the process, be the genius in our doings:

1. Go to a new country or new location, leaving behind the past.

By restarting our life with awareness, we avoid past habits that were limiting and lead every thought from the intent of where we wish to be. Relocation now stimulates the right and left brain as in relating to each and there is much progress from being a seeker to becoming a master.

2. Understand, respect and work the root chakra and complete ourselves.

Although most religions advocate celibacy, the mystical paths of most religions, with special reference to the path of the Siddhars, advocates wise utilization of the root chakra, as in understanding the need for a healthy sexual attitude, healthy relationships, the primal needs of food and sustenance from a point of moderation and Consciousness.

In other words, when we embrace the root chakra, we embrace all the trivialities of life, as in responsibilities. This enables us to exercise the left and right brain in everyday realities, even more.

3. Understanding time as in what we do each moment.

When realizing that we are the Spirit having the human experience, we also understand the Spirit as very ancient and the body as limited in time by a shelf life. In this understanding, is the utilization of each moment exclusively aligned to our highest purpose.

We awaken to time. We realize that time is an experience and each moment of time needs be justified by what we do. The old Zen adage of 'Chopping wood before awakening and chopping wood after awakening' does not hold true.

Once awake, we will want to utilize our time more efficiently by how we act, whether it is in meditation and practices that brings us Harmony or in day to day work that has our heart's intent in it. An awake being, normally, would sooner or later drop out of the rat race of survival mode and instead see each moment of work justifying the highest purpose of existence.

4. Consider this quote by Rumi, 'Everyone has been made for some particular work and the desire for that work has been put in every heart.'

Understand genius as states of joy that we uniquely feel while doing whatever we love doing from our heart and that no one is smarter than another. Everyone has a unique state genius: Take the case of any insect or animal as an example to see how there is a particular thing that every living being has that cannot be replicated by another species.

Likewise, every person has a unique talent waiting to be tapped. This talent or talents are that which each one of us are specially programmed for by destiny. When we find the activity that gives us most joy and understand this as an expression of ourselves that gives us maximum satisfaction, we begin to see sparks of our innate genius awaken. This is the right and left brain now aligning itself through the states of joy in our doing.

5. Consider ourselves a whole being with many spokes in our wheels as multitalented abilities.

Beings like Leonardo Da Vinci are perfect examples, who exemplify the genius in the many levels of accomplishment they were capable of. History notes that Leonardo Da Vinci once wrote a bio of himself to the countess of Turin while seeking to be invited. In his bio, he lists over 25 different facets of himself, each facet shows amazing genius.

Today we know Leonardo Da Vinci as a talented master artist. Leonardo Da Vinci lists his skill as an artist as the 23rd. This example of Leonardo Da Vinci depicts the mind of a person awake to understand the wholeness of being and the potency to be the master in many abilities. The ability to do inspired work or play from the perspective of seeing ourselves as immensely huge beings exercises the bridge between the right and left brain.

6. Understanding the journey into vaster and ever vaster Consciousness is never ending, while delving into the joy and bliss factor of this inner journey through the mind and beyond the mind each day.

After the initial experience of awakening, the journey has just started! The right brain is forever thriving on more and more stimulation for connectivity to God/Source/Infinity or whatever we could call this. The Sages of the east call this, yoga, the sacred union between individual ego and Source.

When we awaken to this heightened state of joy, we then set a daily discipline to have more of this each day. This joy and bliss of love in the yoga tradition is called Bhakti. Adi Sankara, one of India's most revered masters mentions, 'When there is more of Bhakti, there is more of wisdom.' This equation of Bhakti and wisdom translates as superior intellect and genius in doings.

It does not matter for us to feel awake or not awake and compare ourselves with anyone. All that matters for ourselves is to hold on to our own experiences, starting with understanding states of joy and bliss in our daily practice of going inward, be it praying, meditation, contemplation or any practice that gives us joy, like dancing, yoga or even cooking and acknowledging that bliss and joy state to be that of genius.

Slowly, we will set our discipline to have more joy as we are on the journey through Consciousness

Awake, the vastness of Consciousness now serves as profound realities that fulfill and inspire us. In the process of our own awakening to higher Consciousness, humanity, too, transforms itself to the ingrained nature of Peace, Harmony, tranquility, love, freedom and abundance.

AHIMSA PRINCIPLE: YOGIC INSIGHT ON AHIMSA

Ahimsa is the practice of not harming or killing any living being. Yet, the Dalai Lama said, 'Forgiveness doesn't mean forgetting what happened. If something is serious and it is necessary to take counter-measures, you have to take counter-measures.'

This is common sense in the reality in which we live today. Known for his practice and advocacy of Ahimsa, this statement from the Dalai Lama might seem contradictory. There is however a deeper Yogic wisdom to the principle of Ahimsa.

Our world is energy. Balancing the world is about balancing energy. There are three basic states of energy called gunas, which can shed light on the applicability of the Ahimsa principle in our times.

The first is the Tamasic mind, which means darkness and is a mind characterized by ignorance, violence, and destructive tendencies. The second is the Rajasic mind, which is characterized by action and momentum fueled by greed and selfishness. The third is the Sattvic mind that is pure, illumined, and without impurities. The Sattvic mind is rooted in the principles of Ahimsa.

When World War II broke out, Mahatma Gandhi wrote to Hitler, trying to persuade Hitler away from being an aggressor; these letters reached Hitler just before his invasion of Poland. Hitler chose to ignore the letters and simply went ahead, invading and annexing Poland. Gandhi's Ahimsa principle had fallen on deaf ears. At the same time, Gandhi was of the opinion that the Jews who were being persecuted by the Nazis 'should submit themselves meekly and as Satyagrahis (spiritual warriors) will triumph'. Today, now that the world knows for sure the determined evil intent behind the Nazi regime, we understand that Gandhi's Ahimsa principle would have failed to stop the massacre of Jews. In fact it would have aided the Nazi authorities in achieving their aim of mass murder of the Jews.

From the Yogic point of view, Nazi Germany was in the grip of Tamas. Britain was Rajasic and the non-violent India headed by Gandhi was Sattvic. According to the Yogic perception of the Gunas, Tamas can be effectively dealt with only through the Rajasic nature. Likewise, the Rajasic nature can be overcome only by the Sattvic nature. In other words, it was only through the violence of war (Rajasic energy) that Britain, America and the other fourteen allied countries could defeat Nazi Germany and Imperial Japan. Likewise, it was exclusively Sattvic non-violent India, following the Ahimsa principle that could overcome the colonial British rule of Rajasic nature. It is important to see human realities for what they are: states of energy. Now we understand why the Dalai Lama said what he said.

The Islamic State, Hamas and Al Qaida are sad symptoms of the increasing face of avidya (ignorance of Oneness) that is stalking humanity today in the form of terrorism and war lords. When bin Laden was in his destructive element, facing him with the principle of Ahimsa would not have worked. Terrorists and extremists such as bin Laden often desire to achieve the status of martyr and receive other heavenly rewards by using violence.

The disease to be addressed is the advocacy of intolerance, violence, barbaric punishments and male dominant belief-systems that justify the likes of Osama bin Laden, the Taliban and the growing fundamentalism around the globe.

Wishing away this growing threat by standing on the principles of Ahimsa is questionable, as we are dealing with Tamas that cannot be suppressed directly by the Sattvic nature. Quite simply, Rajas will have to be employed to limit Tamas

– and Rajas means resistance and counter-action. This isn't justification of violence or 'an eye for an eye' – this is simply saying that, giving in without resistance (Ahimsa) is not the way to go and action has to be taken when we are faced with Tamas (violence).

WEALTH OF CONSCIOUSNESS

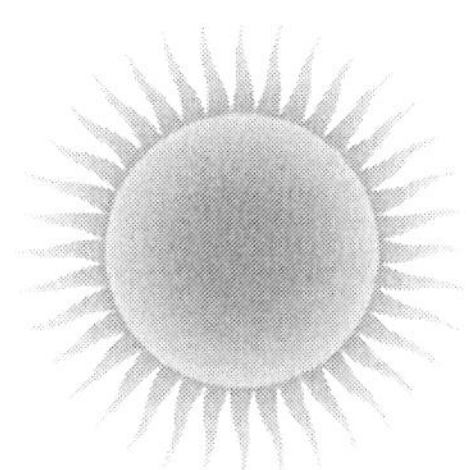

Consciousness and wealth – spiritual and material – are not just related, but are interwoven as one flowing energy field. When there is Peace and Harmony, abundance of all good things flow naturally, not just for individuals, but also for whole nations. The impact of the collapse of the US economy has had global implications; US debt is $14.6 trillion and climbing. That is roughly $47,000 debt for every US citizen.

Is there a need to be worried? What will happen next to the nation, to global economics and our own individual reality? What will happen if a totalitarian regime armed with economic strength gains the upper hand to threaten our individual freedom?

These questions and thoughts can be brought to the right perspective if we can understand Consciousness as being the wealth that will always gain precedence over any temporary upheavals.

If we can gain insights into the history of Consciousness, we know we will not fail. We are Consciousness that is victorious. Always!

India had been an economic super power for over 2000 years prior to being colonized by the British Empire. At that time, the entire global economy was less than 50% of that of India – the global economy of that period of course included a relatively un-developed China. Compare this to the 50-year maximum time of the 'super-power' status of the USA that in its heyday constituted only 15% of the global economy.

This enormous wealth of India was driven for centuries by a foundation of Harmony from within. Economic strength grew due to this inner Harmony, the result of the absence of wars, especially in South India. Isolated from invasions for thousands of years thanks to the three oceans to the south and the Himalayas to the north, the Indian subcontinent sustained a society where spirituality was a foundation on which enterprise prospered along with science. The Indian subcontinent provided and still provides the sustaining and nurturing environment to not just a few spiritual seekers, but to over three million sadhus, or spiritual recluses.

Consider these facts of an inherent Consciousness:

- During its years as a 'super-power', India did not invade/plunder or evangelize any of its neighboring countries. All of its neighbors were trading partners, and culture and philosophy flowed naturally. Wars were civilized! Wars were fought within the Indian subcontinent with the intent of no civilian casualties, no killing prisoners of war, and hostilities would cease every evening to tend to the wounded etc. Sadly, this code changed with the advent of the Muslim invaders from 1200 A.D. onwards; they came to plunder India and forcefully impose Islam on the conquered people, while committing atrocities that violated the ethics of war. With the advent of British imperialism, all ethics of war were done with.

- Throughout India's history, anyone and everyone stepping on the shores of India was treated as welcomed guests of honor. 'The guest is our God-Artithi Devam'- is part of the ingrained culture that still richly exists in most India today. India is the only country that not only welcomed the Jews, but also ensured that they were protected, and their trade was encouraged. This is exactly the policy that the East India Company took advantage of to later colonize India.

- Mother India faced over six hundred years of Islamic rule with forced religious conversions and destruction of over 30000 Temples and shrines, followed by three hundred years of European colonialization. The inherent culture, language and religion did not suffer too big a dent. Nearly all of India's native languages (over 150 distinct languages) remain. Most of the indigenous cultures across vast country remain- barring Islamic majority states. Mother India as Hinduism survived the impact of history as Consciousness cannot be trampled upon. (Compare this to Latin America/Africa/Middle East and other colonial dominated part of the world where the original language, religion and culture of entire nations were obliterated completely and replaced by that of the conquerors).

- When Mahatma Gandhi started his non-violent freedom struggle in India, the British felt threatened almost immediately, as the vast majority of the Indian population were agreeable to the concept of Ahimsa — non-hurting, non-harming and non-killing as a non-violent path to attaining freedom. Yet Ahimsa was a new concept, untried in human history. Before Gandhi, Indians had struggled for freedom through violent means. What baffled the British and the press was how, without modes of modern communication, huge crowds would form and wait for hours before Gandhi arrived at any destination. The freedom movement had the whole of India responding to Gandhi's call to be the 'soul-force' from the beginning —this eventually led to Britain's decision to leave India as a friend. Consciousness still won over steel, guile and greed.

- Today, Consciousness, the gift of Mother India, triumphs through yoga- through each of us.

When the British got their first administrative hold on the Indian subcontinent, starting with what is known today as Tamil Nadu, the British knew that they would conquer the rest of India with the financial 'profits' they made – they knew that they had plundered the world's richest region. In 1803, the East India Trading Company (later taken over by the British government) made a profit of 13 million pounds (approx $5 billion in today's value) from a territory which later expanded to almost 25 times this size. This 'profit' compounded each year by a minimum of 100% and sometimes by as much as 1000%, year after year as newer territories were annexed – until the entire Indian subcontinent was under the Empire. India gained Independence in 1947, but not before India had footed the entire bill for the UK's First and Second World Wars as well as all the other wars fought by the British. If we sum up the amount of wealth taken out of India directly and indirectly from 1800 to 1947, by comparison, the current US debt of $15 trillion is minuscule.

Consciousness, however, moves in cycles and is not the monopoly of any one culture or country. The ancient Consciousness of the Indian subcontinent is embedded in the science of yoga, meditation and the essence of realizing oneness — Ahimsa. This cycle of goodness for Consciousness is now beginning again. The enormous wealth that was with India in the form of stored Consciousness through being a super-power for over 2000 years was not depleted, because wealth, spiritual and material, is created through Consciousness.

When we meditate, do yoga or do any practice that calms the mind to Harmony, we experience Peace. Thoughts from a mind of Harmony are always innovative, abundant, nurturing and inspiring.

As thoughts of the Sages from the East, we wish all to know that even $100 trillion is still minuscule compared to collective Consciousness that can be transformed to abundant material realities in a moment.

The immenseness of spiritual abundance is a power that has come of age, and no one person, no nation and no ignorance can stop its manifestation to be the radiance of material abundance.

May we all evolve in our awakening to the Harmony of oneness behind each thought. May we all unfold abundant realities in our lives that fulfill, inspire and bless us with well-being, contentment and enterprise that enables the goodness of abundance.

SECTION C :

INTERVIEW WITH NANDHIJI

Questions by Sri Prateeka Ananda:

Q. In India people understand the reason to have a guru. In the West it is not well known. What is the purpose of having a Guru and how does that help you?

A. The 'Guru' is really the wisdom behind our mind and each thought. Books we read, the company we keep, Mother Nature – anything or anybody who influences us is our Guru. In the spiritual journey, a Guru is the one who opens us to the higher self, to God as the external Source of all things, and to the God within.

As in the Biblical element of 'Holy Son, Holy Ghost and Holy Father', we see the Guru as the Holy Son who awakens us to our own soul as the Holy Ghost, and the infinite Source as our Holy Father. In our Siddhar knowing, we understand and realize our Guru to be the grace that burns away our ignorance, and in a moment, enables us to be the higher conscious being, awake. When we awaken, we are in gratitude to the one who paved our way to Source, as the Guru. The Guru then becomes the epicenter of our worship, to receive the constant grace of ever expanding Consciousness – as the awareness beyond the mind that continually guides us. The external Guru awakens us to our inner Guru, self-knowledge, self-realization and our awareness.

Q. How does one recognize a true Guru? Are there any tests we should use?

A. Any person, book or even animal that awakens us to our own innate wisdom to connect with Source or to understand ourselves as Source, is our Guru, fit to be held in reverence. For example, Christ, in the Bible, is a Guru. The Guru in human form is the one who transforms our mind and its realities through mantras, talk or presence. There is however a unique Guru for each of us based on our own uniqueness of being. The inner-most desires to connect with Source manifests the specific Guru who appears in our life, aligning our own primal need. If there is a 'test', it works both ways – to ascertain if the Guru is of the Consciousness we can relate to; and a test for ourselves, to see if we are able to ascertain and live up to the wisdom of a Guru whom we can hold in respect, love and reverence.

Q. What is meditation and why is it so beneficial?

A. The mind and all thought patterns hold the momentum of the past that is attuned to 'karma'– the sum total of the past reflected in the 'Now'; karma is a law of reaping a reality – that which has been sowed, those actions and thoughts of the past. When we meditate or pray we step outside the mind and experience being the vastness or void as in the Buddhist path and/or as the Spirit as in the Hindu pathway. On the rooftop of the mind, beyond the chatter of thoughts, we are liberated of the past and its momentum. Above on the mind's rooftop, we begin to realize the Oneness of ourselves with All to align into the 'Now'. A meditator is able to come into the 'Now' with ease, and this enables the mind to be stress-free, intuitive and able to create thoughts that are not from the momentum of past patterns of the mind.

In our Siddhar experimental wisdom, we describe Source/God as our own experience of bliss. When we meditate, we tap into the higher spiritual Self we truly are, and in the physical realities attune ourselves as Spirit having a human experience. Absence of stress, ability to be in bliss, inspired with the higher wisdom and a sense of wholeness are but just a few benefits of meditation that is causal to good health, healthy relationships, successful career and a life of fulfillment and love.

Q. Is spirituality even relevant in our time? And, if so, what would a person gain by becoming more spiritual?

A. What we mean by 'spirituality' is awakening to who we really are and realizing the Oneness of the Divine. Spirituality is also a distillation of Consciousness, and this Consciousness has a flow. humanity has attained 'critical mass' where we now have a large and growing number of awakened and conscious beings around the globe. This Consciousness flows as a candle lighting more candles. These are the beautiful moments for all of humanity to be the recipients of this blessed flow of Consciousness.

In awakening to be spiritual we understand the Divine to be both innumerable names and the nameless. As we surrender our mind, our thoughts, our worries and anxieties to Source to attain a meditative state of mind, we become the epicenter, like the Sun, with the mind and all realities revolving around ourselves. By surrendering our mind and all the mundane to Source, from being the slave of the mind, we become the Emperor who manifests perfect Harmony-aligned realities.

Q. Is there any reason for people who do not believe in God to meditate?

A. An atheist might actually be a better meditator than a person who clings on to the past, sometimes to imperfect beliefs in God and religion. Above the mind's rooftop is the liberation from thoughts and the knowing of ourselves as vast beings, but also inter-connected to one another and Source. There are no expectations or even desires other than wanting more of bliss and joy that accompanies this state of mind. Gautama Buddha was asked about God. His response was silence. For an atheist, meditation is the realization of the vastness within and this realization is by itself 'Spiritual'.

Q. Can an atheist who practices meditation gain realization?

A. History has many higher conscious beings like Plato, Socrates and far too many to name, who attained 'realization' through the starting point of disbelief in existing religious tenets. Buddhism stems from the atheistic principle to come to the point of realizing higher Consciousness as infinity and mindfulness. Meditation is a perfect tool of Consciousness for anyone.

Q. Are we entering into a new age of spirituality? Are we making the transition into an age of more light?

A. Every master of Consciousness of the past came to planet Earth to grow humanity by leaving seeds of Consciousness. These seeds of Consciousness have grown and multiplied to the numbers we are experiencing today. Even the internet and this age of information aids in the spread of Consciousness. Yes, whether we are all ready for this 'New Age of Spirituality/Consciousness' or not, Consciousness flows and it will transform humanity as an idea whose time has come.

Q. Was Jesus Christ a Yogi? What about Prophet Mohammed?

A. A 'Yogi' is the one who has merged himself/herself with Source. The proof of Jesus is the beautiful life mesSage of love, tolerance and compassion he left behind for us, as effective tools of Consciousness. Of course, Jesus was a Yogi! Prophet Mohammed was also a Yogi whose unity with Source flowed with the powerful wisdom of his times – a flow of higher Consciousness in a medieval age of conflict.
When we connect to Source, we are the Yogi. We are able then to tap into the 'Now' that enables us to flow in the highest wisdom that is more perfect than all of history's Holy Scriptures. But this 'wisdom' we flow with is exclusively good for ourselves and may not be perfect wisdom for another. Therefore, it is good to write our own Koran/Bible and follow each word by our self and never enforce it upon others; each human has an innate inner wisdom that is truer for them. Each of us awake is the Prophet.

Q. Most religions teach that their path is the only true path. What does Nandhiji say about this?

A. The word 'religion' comes from the action of being 'religious', in following a set of rules to attain proximity to Source – much like driving directions. After attaining proximity to Source, what use are the driving directions? From here, what we each uniquely do is our own personal religion. The path to Source is through states of joy that ultimately liberate us to the same experiences cherished by each 'Prophet' of the past.

Follow the life mesSage of each Prophet – to never follow the previous Prophet, but be liberated by the wisdom of Source to be in the 'Now'; follow the one and only true path, the path of our Heart aligned to our own reasoning that is causal to more bliss, joy, freedom, love and fulfillment. Any doctrine, beliefs or even religion that does not align to our own reasoning, logic and heart's wisdom does not serve in enhancing Consciousness.

Q. Why does Hinduism have so many gods/goddesses? Is it the same for Siddhar wisdom? Why does the West have so few Gods?

A. In India, God/Source is worshipped and seen in everything and in all aspects of life. From the disease of leprosy to the herbal healing plant tulasi, there is a facet of the Divine dedicated to it. Swamy Vivekananda, the first of the masters of higher Consciousness who came to the West, asked: 'If a cat had a God, what God would it be?' Each one of us has a unique mind and our own concept of God.

In India there are over a million forms of God to choose from – you can still be an atheist and still be a 'Hindu', as evidenced by the cat that visualizes its particular God as another cat. For a Yogi and the essence of Hinduism however, the inner journey realizes us to the One that is all – called

Brahman, Paramatman, Siva, Easwara. Source, or God, is realized as the One who takes countless forms and is the nameless form within all things and all living creatures; this is the central theme of Hinduism. The greeting 'Namaste' means, 'I worship the Divine in You'.

In the West, the concept of a monotheist God, together with a rigid code of conduct and an exclusive pathway to God via the leadership of religious Prophets is part of a process initiated by the Prophet Abraham. Religion in the West has been accompanied by violence, hate and cruelty, as each new religion hybridized the 'mine is the only way' to even greater exclusivity; in the last of recent history's newest offshoots, Islam, and its Prophet declared that he was the last one around. The One God theme of religious exclusivity made this curse of humanity more convenient.

In the Siddhar wisdom, we wake up to the oneness in all living things. This wisdom awakens us to the concept of Ahimsa – non-hurting, non-harming, non-killing, tolerance and basic goodness as we recognize the Divine in all living creatures. The Siddhars see the universality of God, of God as male and female aspect entwined together. A Siddhar Sage understands the multitude of Divinity in each unique form – so for a Siddhar to worship Allah and/or Christ is as normal as worshiping any other form of God.

Q. Generally, Western religions have shunned the idea of idol worship. Why do people worship statues in the Indian traditions? Is there really any benefit in this?

A. A Muslim prays in the direction of Mecca; other religions worship a picture/idol of Christ in a church. We build churches and temples and mosques. All of these things are deigned to focus the mind on God. The external and internal focal points are necessary so the mind can funnel all thoughts to singularity.

When we wake up to realize Source/God, we begin to understand that the vastness of infinity of God is too limiting, even to name. Relating to the Divine in grounded reality, we see the Divine in all things. When a Yogi places an idol as a focus of worship, he or she is invoking the Divine to be the form represented. When children in India are named after a God, when we call that child, we are invoking the Divine. From a more rational approach, when we bring focus to any specific facet of God/Source and dwell each thought on that form, we transform to that form. This explains how worshipers of Christ have stigmata-like occurrences.

With focus and intent on the form/idol we can bring our mind to stillness, the essence of meditation and prayers. With dedication, focus and intent, the form we hold in reverence to the Divine awakens the formless attributes within us.

Q. Could Nandhiji explain why the Gods act so strangely in the various stories in Indian tradition? They cheat on one another. They curse one another. They have affairs. What is the meaning behind this?

A. Ultimately, if we see each human as God, then a good question is: why is there still so much ignorance? However, the right question to ask is: 'When one sees God in another, is that person less prone to violence, hatred and intolerance?' The answer would be yes.

Most Hindu stories, like most scripture-based stories in the religions of the world, reveal a conflict between the human and the Divine, as to what is the correct moral code. These scriptural stories can be defined as the fight of Consciousness/good versus ignorance/the bad. This moral code changes with each culture, with time and the prevailing circumstances. When we look back into stories of the past from any culture around the world, we see the good, the bad and the ugly and yet within all this is the thread of Consciousness that underpins the moral within the story.

Ultimately, we come to our own inner realization of the highest wisdom: to do for others what we might for ourselves – non-harming, non-hurting, truthfulness etc., as we understand stories of scriptures to represent the growing Consciousness of humanity.

What drew Nandhiji to the mystical component of Hinduism?

A. Nandhijii's first childhood experience at the age of five was to experience the Divine in the human form in his pilgrimage with his father. Later, growing up with introspective questions in a boarding school environment, it was challenging to reconcile the inner-most knowing and the absolute practical world, with classmates who were so far from any trace of Consciousness. In those days, Nandhiji would often go to the isolated forest and cemetery areas of his school and sit quietly, or start a small fire, often times not understanding its purpose; it simply felt good. Through these moments, there was a knowing that beyond all the 'realities' experienced, there was the mystical truth out there waiting to be connected with, and that this 'wisdom' needed a Guru.

Later, aged 16, Nandhiji met his first 'Guru', Lewis, from London, who exposed Nandhiji to the mystical aims of Hinduism from a theoretical perspective. It was however, through a near death experience, aged 26, that Nandhiji woke up to understand that all he was seeking in the past had unraveled itself as an inner journey to undertake. The moment this inner journey began, Nandhiji's external life slowly dissolved away – his family, his business, his friends. Even as the external world dissolved away, a newer world of awe, mysticism and miracles unfolded not as incidents alone, but as each day's experience. It was then that Nandhiji realized that this was exactly the experience he sought as a little child and he had found it as a continuation of a journey of many previous lives in the 'Now'.

Q. Hinduism has the Veda, Christians the Bible, Judaism the Torah, but what is the Siddhar principal text? Is it the Palm leaf manuscript, The Siddhar Project Dr. Ganapathy works on?

A. The Siddhar lineage of Gurus is unbroken and goes back several thousands of years. The teachings of the Siddhars however did not base itself much on written scriptures, because some of the Siddhar Sages were uneducated. The Siddhar teachings, transforming grace and the ancient wisdom was imparted through resonance as mantra, 'deeksha' and physical one-on-one teachings – this woke up the seeker to understand and climb upwards to self-realization. The Siddhars proclaim the self-realized truth of each to be truer than any written scripture. Thousands of years of Guru's grace was conveyed through the 'awakening' resonance and practices which transferred Consciousness, while the disciple surrendered his/her mind, thoughts and realities in humility to the Guru who imparted this grace. Much of the Siddhar wisdom holds many effective tools of Consciousness and its mastery requires a spiritually mature aspirant, so that there is responsibility in the usage of such powerful wisdom. It was for this reason that all Siddhars wrote their teachings as Divine poetry in the 'Sandhya' language (also called the twilight language) that can be understood differently from each stage of Consciousness, i.e., a person with hardly any Consciousness will not be able to understand even the elementary steps to take, and the literal translation of Siddhar poetry will make no sense at all. However, for a person of higher Consciousness, the writings are much like a recipe with all the readily available ingredients such as knowledge of breath, knowledge of each chakra etc., to cook the most amazing inner reality.

Q. What is Nandhiji's favorite mantra?

A. This is a difficult question to answer as the mantra we may choose to recite this moment would be different from the one we chanted previously, and yet each mantra at the moment of chanting is the most favorite of the moment. However, looking deeper into the word 'Mantra', we might seek the essence of the sacred sound to understand that which can be imparted to enable each to be Angelic; to understand the self as Si, the vast Spirit/God we are, and Va as the experience, the feminine aspect, the two breaths of the left and right, within ourselves as in the simple but most potent mantra 'Siva Sivaa'. It is no surprise to see Siva Sivaa mentioned on nearly all Lord Siva temples in South India as the Siddhar teaching awakening us to know that we are God having a human experience.

Questions by Ganganath and Tara:

Q. Who is Lord Siva from a Siddhar perspective?

A. Lord Siva is the final point of infinity, Source, that is experienced each moment by the Siddhar Yogi as bliss. This bliss is explained by the Yogis as experiencing the Infinite Presence as the higher vibrations. The Yogi realizes Lord Siva as the essence of himself as the awakened Soul that is present in all living beings. Lord Siva is the infinite being present within an atom and the energy within nothingness – the energy that is understood as the dance that causes bliss, the vibratory state of being. The Siddhar Sages understand Lord Siva as the One, the multiple realities we experience. Lord Siva is the ultimate identity to seek within ourselves that we can reflect as the external world.

Q. Who is Lord Ganesh from a Siddhar perspective?

A. We can understand Lord Ganesh as from the mythological story related to his creation.
The story:
Goddess Sakti felt her privacy was being invaded by Lord Siva, when he entered her house at will. Out of dirt, she created a son, Lord Ganesh, to guard the entrance. When Lord

Siva came back to enter Goddess Sakti's house, he was blocked by the boy, who refused to allow Lord Siva access. Infuriated by this boy who refused to budge despite the cajoling, rewards and threats by Lord Siva, a battle ensued. Lord Siva in anger, not knowing the boy to be his son, cut the boy's head off. Goddess Sakti was enraged and Lord Siva came to regret his action. To placate Goddess Sakti, an elephant's head was placed on the boy – he would become the elephant-headed God who was now given all the authority and responsibility to guard the entrance of Goddess Sakti's house forever, as Lord Ganesh.

Goddess Sakti is Mother Kundalini, the inner fire, and Lord Siva is the power of awareness. Lord Ganesh is the root chakra that stands as guard and as guide, opening the door to our awakening. The human body of Lord Ganesh represents the rare fortunate birth as human, and the elephant head represents the primal energies of sexuality, the five senses and the survival instinct. All the primal energies and desires are transmuted upwards to align with the highest purpose of our human birth through the grace of Lord Ganesh – hence, he is called the Lord of the Journey, the Dissolver of Obstacles (obstacles on our spiritual path and external realities) and the son of Lord Siva, the infinite, and Goddess Sakti, the energy of realities experienced. With Lord Ganesh of the root chakra's grace, we awaken our Mother Kundalini to unite with Lord Siva, the highest wisdom.

Q. What does 'Aum Namah Sivaya' actually mean?

A. The mantra Aum Namah Sivaya means, I worship Source dwelling in the primordial infinity. Aum is the primordial infinity of Source. Namah is surrender/dissolve/beyond ego. Si is the Spirit/Soul/Supreme Being and Va is the experience/Goddess. Ya represents the 'knowing', the wisdom of experiencing Source union as in the third eye.

Q. What is the significance of a 'devotional lamp?'

A. Ultimately, the only truth of our spiritual journey is the lamp alight within. This lamp, the inner fire, is the essence of passionate union between our awareness and Source that enables our devotional joys. Our Sages teach that the most potent blessing to receive is the fervor to seek more of Source and more lighting this flame within, the devotional lamp. When we light a lamp in physical reality, we are assisting the manifestation of our inner lamp, the devotional lamp.

Q. What is the Siddhar definition of a 'Yogi?'

A. A Yogi is a person who is not only connected to Source, as in the daily disciplines of practices to unite with Source, but also is aware of each moment and each breath of the sacred Source union.

Q. What is a 'cosmic beggar?'

A. A Yogi's quest and destination is to be whole and in wholeness and in attaining this state of wholeness, the Yogi understands each moment as a miracle and every activity as a Divine gift. The Yogi understands himself/herself to be a cosmic beggar receiving grace and realities from Source as an instrument of the Divine.

Q. What is meant by 'be the Prophet?

A. A 'Prophet' is understood to be an advocate of God, one who is Source connected. This terminology brought much sorrow and pain for humanity in the Western and Middle Eastern civilizations, as it is associated with crusades and jihads, as each Prophet insisted on the exclusive nature of their truth. In Eastern history, anyone insisting on being called a Prophet, in the exclusive sense of 'pathway', would have been ignored simply because of the underlying ego within such assumptions.

When we wake up, we too are directly in union with Source/Infinity/God/Consciousness. This 'waking up' is the birthright of all humans. We then need to understand ourselves as Prophet and learn from the life story of each Prophet with this first truth: No Prophet ever followed the previous Prophet. As Prophet, let us write our own codes of disciplines as our personal Bible/Koran and let us never enforce these rules on any other, other than ourselves. This age of Consciousness now enables us to make this declaration – be the Prophet.

Q. What is the significance of a mantra?

A. When we meet an enlightened person and seek blessings, everything we ask for is small and temporary, compared to asking for a piece of that Consciousness that makes a person 'enlightened'. This Consciousness is transferred by way of the mantra. The mantra is the sound resonance that carries with it the embedded grace of all the masters who chanted the mantra previously. When the mantra is chanted, the vibrations within the resonance of the mantra carry our level of Consciousness to that of the mantra frequencies. The place where thoughts emerge, Consciousness shifts. We think from a higher place. Each mantra however is unique in its resonance and our own intent while reciting each mantra works alongside in the inner journey through the mind and beyond. Our realities align to where we are thinking from.

Q. What is the role of sensuality in Siddhar philosophy – are Siddhars celibate?

A. In the Siddhar philosophy, the idea of 'natural flow' is important in for our evolution. The root chakra is important, as it is from the roots that the inner fire is built as a foundation to the spiritual practice –- hence the name 'tantiram' is given to the South Indian Siddhar teachings. The Siddhars did not conform to any of society's moral values. Some Siddhars write of attaining several spiritual progresses through making love and they teach several love-making techniques for attaining specific goals. Other Siddhars advocate celibacy. A person can be celibate and practice the tantiram teachings, understanding all of reality as the spiritual journey within.

Q. What are the chakras and the significance of each?

A. Each chakra is a bed of Consciousness from where we experience a specific level of thinking and a specific reality. For a Yogi, each chakra is a platform; we climb from one platform to another to rise in Consciousness as the fulfillment of each chakra enables the chakras above to blossom. Each chakra is therefore like a key that opens the lock to the chakra above. Our meditative journey ascends through the chakras to then be the whole; we are like cosmic monkeys, jumping from one chakra 'branch' to another until we reach the place of inspired alignment with Source.

Q. How do the Siddhars see Christ?

A. Christ is a master/Guru. Siddhars see Christ as one of the forebears of Consciousness who was way ahead of his time and was therefore crucified. Christ, as with all enlightened masters of the past, has an eternal Consciousness; when we connect with that Consciousness, as in prayers, meditation or contemplation, we are bound to be blessed with the grace of that higher Consciousness. However, the teachings imparted by Christ then, as recorded in the Bible and the teachings of Christ the man, although fundamentally the same, would differ in substance. For instance, although Christ talked of love and non-violence for one human to another, the Consciousness prevalent in the society at that time was limited.

Were Christ here now, his message of love and non-violence for all living beings would not fall on deaf ears, as society's Consciousness has grown and Christ Consciousness too, would have expanded even further. So for a Yogi, Christ is Consciousness and this Consciousness can be attained s.

Q. What are states of Consciousness?

A. After 'awakening', our true journey through Consciousness has begun. This journey takes us higher and higher, and there is no ending, although with each progression we become more and more God-like. Everything – even an atom has Consciousness – and it is only the level of Consciousness that differs. A human could have the Consciousness of an animal or that of an Angel. It is the gifted human who can choose where in Consciousness they wish to be.

Once on the journey through higher Consciousness, the state of Turiya – super Consciousness – unravels. Even within the Turiya state, there are said to be 18 levels, and yet, trying to define Turiya is like trying to ascertain the size of the known and unknown universe.

Q. Why do ascetics take a vow of poverty? Is this the only way to enlightenment?

A. The process of seeking begins with disillusionment. Disillusionment with the realities of life, to attachments, money and security. In the beginning we feel like 'nothing in this world belongs to me' as a natural adherence to the vow of poverty. This vow often leads to becoming a renunciant (in India, the sanyasi). On our path to attain wholeness, we understand the need for moderation and we develop the wisdom to know the ways of karma and dharma. We understand that our human purpose is solely to evolve; to do that, we need to do dharma and we also realize that we can negate the law of karma by doing dharma. After attaining more wholeness, we see the world from a new perspective: 'the whole world is mine and I am a part of this world'. At this point we have graduated to be the raja-sanyasi – the king who is renunciant. At this point we are comfortable with money, as we see money as energy with which goodness can be enhanced, as in dharma. We are now like a duck in water, swimming in the realities, floating abundantly while not being attached to a single drop of water.

Questions by Najla Devi:

Q. What is the significance of shaving off one's hair?

A. The hair carries the energies of our past. Shaving off the hair is symbolic to letting go of the past.

Q. What is 'tummo'?

A. Tummo is the inner fire kindled by the Yogi that enables the generation of heat. With tummo, a Yogi is able to withstand freezing temperatures without wearing any clothes. Tummo is especially relevant in tantric traditions as it involves awakening the root chakra fire and growing this fire as awareness within each breath.

There are two dimensions within 'tummo'. One form of tummo is the ability to go beyond bodily limits when cold, by generating the inner fire's warmth. The other form of tummo is in being able to sit under the hot sun for hours together enabling the 'cool' within the body to withstand scorching heat.

Q. What is 'Yogic focus?'

A. Within the meditative state, the Yogi can focus the mind at a single point, a point that contains infinity. Holding the single thought as Yogic focus is much like holding the vastness of infinity with no thoughts. Both are the same ends of the Yogic process of focus and both lead to experiencing 'the dance within stillness'. It is this Yogic focus that enables a Yogi to sit in solitude for days, if not months and years together, absorbed in the dance within stillness.

Q. What is the significance of Lord Vishnu in Siddhar philosophy?

A. Lord Vishnu is an important facet of a meditative trinity for a Siddhar Yogi. This meditative trinity is: Lord Siva as the infinite absolute; Goddess Sakti as our inner fire; and Mother Kundalini and Lord Vishnu is our mind awake as awareness.

When we invoke the blessings of Lord Vishnu, we understand it to be the attainment of grace of each thought from an empowered mind, which guides us beyond the zone of thoughts. It is the mind that nourishes and sustains us. Awake, the mind is Lord Vishnu, the awareness and mindfulness.

Q. What is the significance of the 'ego' in spiritual growth?

A. It is our ego that brings us back to this birth, and it is ego that gives form and shape to realities. As we become more aware of our true nature, ego dissolves away, as the veil that was between us and Source. Each layer of evolution has different ego patterns arising. A Yogi is careful in dissolving ego at all levels, as ego blocks Source. The higher we climb, different egos arise, such as spiritual ego. Spiritual ego is more dangerous than any lower forms of ego as it can lead to a greater fall. It is for this rational reason that Siddhars prefer to remain anonymous or disguised while in society. The hallmark of a Siddhar is humility and lack of ego.

Q. Discuss the Siddhar principles of gratitude.

A. Siddhars understand each emotion to have a specific energy. Gratitude has one of the highest energies, and paves way to more sublime thoughts. At all times, Siddhars live in the field of gratitude, acknowledging the wholeness and fullness of the moment. Gratitude is the nature of living in the 'Now'.

Q. What is Guru's grace?

A. The one who paves the way to Source is the Guru. This may be a book, a movie or a person. In the pathway of the Siddhars, the ultimate gift of Source is in having a Guru guide us. When the Yogi recites the mantra, prays and meditates revering the Guru, the Yogi is connecting to the Guru and his/her ancient lineage, and is in the flow of grace- just as the Guru before sat invoking his/her Guru, grace flows. Siddhar Rajaswamy would say: 'You need to see an enlightened being just once in your lifetime. At any time later, meditate on that enlightened being and he/she will guide you.' This is the grace of the Guru.

Q. Who or what is the supreme Yogi?

A. The Supreme Yogi is the Lord Siva – another name for Source. For a Yogi, attainment of the highest ideal is to be Source, the Supreme Yogi, perpetually one with Source, beyond limits of the human and constantly evolving.

Q. What is tantra and tantiram from the Siddhar perspective?

A. Tantra comes from the word 'Tantiram', which is in reality, the wholeness within that is attained in the perpetual joy through the unending passionate union with the Divine. This passionate union with Source from the wisdom of tantiram involves awakening the root chakra and connecting the root chakra fires with the ecstasy of the crown chakra. The wisdom behind tantiram is: When there is joy, we will set disciplines to attain more joy; attainment of joy is celebration of the Divine. A Siddhar Sage, an adept in tantiram, could also be celibate.

Q. What is the Siddhar concept of manifestation?

A. The more of a no-thought mind there is, the more of a sustained intense single focus is possible. For a Yogi, manifestation comes with ease, as each thought springs from a powerful focus that enables reality to be created. Siddhar mantras manifest whatever the mind seeks due to their potency. The Siddhars utilize this power of manifestation to manifest Source/God, for only this attainment is eternal. Other desires subside and each thought is utilized solely to evolve in the inner world of spirituality and the outer world of humanity, planet Earth and the entire universe.

Q. What is the principle behind Mother Kundalini's grace of bhakti?

A. Bhakti is devotional love, which is also from the Yogic perspective, Mother Kundalini. In other words when we are Source connected, we are awakening our inner fire, Mother Kundalini. The joy of connecting with Source is bhakti, the devotional love. Bhakti, devotional love, is the first nature of a Yogi.

Q. What is meant by 'genius'?

A. When we are enthralled in anything we do, we are stepping out of the mind and out of time and out of human limits. This state is actually the realm of the Yogi – the Turiya state. At this point, we are driven by the joys of doing and we do not identify ourselves as the doer. Perfection flows naturally from whatever we do, much like an artist creating a masterpiece. This is the 'genius' that we awaken.

Q. Define 'time' from a Siddhar perspective.

A. When we are in the mind, we experience realities and time. When we see time as a reality experienced by the mind, we also understand ourselves trapped within the 24 hour cycle of day and night, within good and bad moods, within the sleep, dream and awake states, and the process of aging. When meditating, we step out of the mind to experience timelessness as the state of Turiya. For Yogis who are often in states of Turiya, in timelessness, realities can be shaped as time. For instance, in the 'Now' moment, a Yogi will manifest all realities to ensure Peace, Harmony and joy in order to bring all the experience of timelessness within time.

Time however too is infinitely vast and also infinitely short from the Yogic perspective of realities. So the Yogis advise: 'Live each day as your last, understanding the self as vast as trillions of light years, here to complete a human life that is in time like a blink of the eyelids.'

Q. Discuss reincarnation from a Siddhar perspective.

A. As we see each meditation as death and a rebirth, we recognize the eternity of ourselves as the Soul. When awakening to our truest being, we realize the pattern of our present life running on a momentum generated by the past; this past might not just be the last birth but several births before. In understanding this past momentum, we are able to bring awareness to our karmic patterns while evolving through our action by doing dharma. If we seek this extent of understanding on reincarnation, we awaken to understand the law of karma and we then will carry optimal baggage of thoughts related to our past.

Q. What does it mean 'to be awake'?

A. A beautiful question! To the awakened, the mind and what we perceive through the mind, as in emotions and excitements, is something like a hat that we wear. We wear the mind as a hat, utilizing the mind for its thoughts but understanding we are the infinite being wearing the mind as a hat. We see the mind like a roof top to climb above and understand the expansive nature of Consciousness as in connecting with Source. We realize that in the lows of the mind, such as sorrow, sadness, mood swings and so on, is a perfect wedge of time to dive deep within to connect profoundly with Source. We see ourselves as the witness to world realities. Each moment to us is a lasting infinite moment that is fulfilled in our doings, knowing that we are not the doer. To be awake is to understand ourselves as conscious beings aware of the laws of karma and dharma. We know this human birth to be precious and our reason to be in the physical body is to fulfill our highest purpose; we live each day as our last.

Q. What is the significance of the Lingam and the various Lingams such as Akasha Lingam, Pinda Lingam, and Atma Lingam?

A. As worshipers of Source in its infinite form, we realize the same Source as a form. When we do this, we create the perfect parking space for the mind while meditating. The Lingam is the most perfect symbolic form to represent infinity and the infinite nature of Lord Siva.

Akasha means the sky in its infinity as the universe of universes. Akasha Lingam is the understanding of Lord Siva as the infinite form.

Pinda is the body. When we perceive our body as the shrine that houses Lord Siva, the Supreme Soul awake, we understand ourselves to be the Pinda Lingam.

Atma Lingam is the heart center. When we converge our thoughts to the heart center, we awaken to Lord Siva as the center of the universe.

These three Lingams form an effective meditation technique when bringing our focus to the singular focus of each of the Lingams. The mind is absorbed in the energy field of each Lingam and our awareness becomes that of the One/Source.

Q. What is meant by 'Breath spirit of the Sages'?

A. Breath waves the mind like a flag in the wind. When we invoke our Gurus or any enlightened master of the past or present, we are connecting to the Spirit of that Being through our breath; in the breath beyond breath, we are one and the same Consciousness of the master we invoke.

Sri Ramakrishna Paramahamsa, one of Mother India's realized masters, was asked by his disciple to show God. The saint responded,' Put your head in a bucket of water and do not come up until you have seen God.' What sounds like a joke actually contains the Siddhar wisdom – hold your breath with the intent of invoking the Divine and in the state of breath held, we become naturally connected and one with the Divine we invoke.

Q. What is the breath channel of the Sun and Moon?

A. Our right nostril breath represents the Sun, known as pingala, and the left nostril breath represents the Moon, the ida. During the day, our breath flips to the right nostril five times. When the breath is predominantly in the right nostril, it means our mind is inspired and active and our metabolic level is high. When our breath is towards the left, it indicates that we are tired and we need to sleep and replenish.

Breath controls the mind and our inner journey through Consciousness. A Yogi works alongside the breath and works the breath to align the mind and the breath beyond breath, to the realm of deep meditation.

Mahasivaswamy, a Siddhar Sage who lived in solitude in a forest for more than 35 years would mention to Nandhiji, 'The ida and pingala breath is your second Guru, after your father and mother who are your first of Gurus. When you understand breath as your Guru, utilize breath as a river through which you swim alongside the currents. Soon you realize that you are the river of breath itself through which you swim across to the union of the Sun and the Moon, the state of Samadhi.' Samadhi is the state of absorption into being one with Source with the mind and sometimes the breath, slowing down and entering into timelessness, the Source of inner-most wisdom.

Q. Do Siddhars astral travel?

A. Astral travel is a special ability of a siddhi that nearly anyone can have, should it be desired. For the Siddhars and most seekers, astral travel is meditative tool to visit the sanctum sanctorum of the sacred shrines, temples and our Gurus. In our desire to go to these sacred places, we begin to experience astral travel – the energy of our desire and the grace of the sacred entity pulls us towards this goal.

The more difficult journey is in the physical! Guru Ayya would advise those wanting to spend years in a cave meditating: 'Go by foot from here (South India) visiting every important temple and shrine, all the way to the Himalayas. Travel then to the East and West of Mother India. After this pilgrimage, sit in a cave and digest all the sacredness of the pilgrimage. In your meditation dwell in all the shrines and temples.' Over years of meditation, the mind gains more and more special powers such as astral travel and when utilized to increase your connection with Source, each special ability becomes an asset of growing value.

Q. Is there a particular breathing technique that the Siddhars use to attain higher states of Consciousness?

A. Just as there are many mantras, there are many breathing techniques. Each Siddhar master has his/her own unique breathing techniques.

There is however one breathing technique described by Thirumulanathar, one of the primordial Siddhar Gurus, that is also followed by many Yogis today. And there is the inner

Aum breath – a secretive breathing technique that was taught by Siddhar Mahasivaswamy, which involves awakening the Moon breath, in order to hold the vastness of the Sun breath. Both these breathing techniques are taught by Nandhiji.

Q. What are angels from a Siddhar perspective?

A. The Yogis are pragmatic and practical. There is no belief system other than the wisdom gained of experience. Angels are not a distant truth. Christ, Buddha and each of the masters of Consciousness are Angelic beings. Even when alive, the Yogis strive to be Spirit having a human experience. By being the Spirit having the human experience, the Yogis celebrate being in heaven while in the physical body; in reality they are the Angels, because they are connected with Source. Each master of the past is revolving around Source as an Angel and when we invoke the masters/ gurus, we are connecting to an Angel.

Q. What is the significance of the six pointed star?

A. South India is one of the world's earliest civilizations, living in Peace and Harmony for over three thousand years. South India was guarded by oceans on three sides; in medieval years many kingdoms stood as a buffer between the invasive forces of the North West frontiers of India. South India was the cradle of spirituality and the Tamil language is as old, if not older than Sanskrit.

The origin of worship of Lord Siva and Goddess Sakti began here in South India. The six pointed representation of Lord Muruga, the son of Lord Siva, has been popular historically and is so even today. Representing the union of the sacred triangle of the human and the triangle of the Divine as the son/daughter of Source, the six pointed star represents the sixth sense amongst a host of other attributes.

The six pointed star represents the Guru of all Gurus. Siddhars understand Lord Muruga as the blessings of instant transformation and enlightenment.

Section E :

108 CONSCIOUSNESS SUTRAS

Note on the Consciousness Sutras:

- Read, absorb and digest each Sutra taking as much time as possible. Sutras contain two or more layers of meaning within to tap into.
- These pictures were taken through Nandhiji's journey. Some are his paintings, others are Divine aligned moments captured.
- Below the pictures are further clarifications of the Sutra.

May we empower ourselves climbing above to the blessed states of Consciousness to determine the magnificence of realities for ourselves and humanity!

Consciousness Sutra 1. Awaken the roots to Evolve!

The healthy roots of the inner fire is grace of ascendance.
As the primal elephant energy awakening the angelic human
to unfold magnificent realities of fulfillment, inspiration and
empowerment of enlightenment the lord of the inner journey
is celebrated.
Awakening the inner fire, all karmic obstacles are dissolved
to pave way to the next evolution of humanity in
Consciousness.
The lord of the journey, Siva be.
Be the Prophet. Aum Namah Sivaya

Just before he left his body, Nandhiji asked Mahasivaswamy for a blessing he could gift to humanity. This blessing was: 'May humanity awaken to its roots and the root's Grace.' When Nandhiji asked him for the deeper meaning behind this blessing, he said, 'When humans realize that they must evolve from the roots of existence – finding love, having a family, an inspiring career and all the mundane duties – there is fulfillment that creates the platform to evolve to the next aspiration – to seek the Divine in focus. The evolution of a human to become Angelic begins the moment there is completion on primary levels.

'When humanity as a collective One Consciousness realizes evolution as a part of life's reality, every human is blessed with Grace to evolve and is blessed in Consciousness.'

Consciousness Sutra 2. Awaken Bhakti, Divine Love

In understanding the roots of bhakti as in each day's joy, our Yogic path unfolds the bed of Consciousness – each thought gaining potency.
At the moolam, the root's center is lord of the journey.
The joys of union with the lord of the journey is in breaking coconuts.
Breaking coconuts of ego, limitations, the karma of past, present and future –
we evolve awake to be the immense elephant adorning the human reality.
As inner lamp awakes; we are the oneness that summons the armies of vast reality each breath.
In breathlessness within joys of bhakti, we are the evolving grace of Consciousness representing highest of intents, awakening the roots to all realities.
In Divine love, as Siva be.
Be the Prophet. Aum Namah Sivaya.

Bhakti means Divine Love – the joys we experience when we pray or when we are Source-connected. This love, bhakti, is the single most important Grace we could ever have; it is like the arrow head of ours seeking for Consciousness.
The coconuts are the realities we face and the moments that dissolve when we surrender ourselves to the Divine. Like coconuts cracked open to reveal the purity within ourselves, we crack our past to awaken the crisp new. Our focus on the Lord of the Journey, Ganesh, invokes the energies of clearing obstacles ahead. In our awakening to Grace is the realization of ourselves being the vast elephant-like being as we experience human realities.

With Grace, we manifest magnificent realities.

Consciousness Sutra 3. Flow of Grace

From walking to running
to flying to gliding
is the sacred momentum
that flows to enable work to transform into inspired play
and joyful timelessness of mighty doings in the grace of
flow.
Super-human accomplishments flow as the genius within
and awaken to worship time in each breath.
Be the breathless joys as Siva gliding in time effortlessly.
The sacred flow in time, Siva be
Be the Prophet.
Aum Namah Sivaya

When we are in a state of joy, inspired, we are in the flow. This flow is Goddess Kundalini. We are awake in the intense joys of Mother Kundalini when we are Source-connected as in meditation or when doing our heart's work. When we are in these states of joy and inspiration, we attain the 'flow' that enables the genius within to shine. Understanding Mother Kundalini as the state of joy and as an inner fire is a Yogic knowing, as being aware of each breath as each moment's discipline that sets us free. Work becomes play and our effort becomes efficient.

Consciousness is the Grace that attains the flow of each moment.

Consciousness Sutra 4. Secret of Manifestation

Ease of manifestation begins with intensity of
desireless desire brought to focus with gratitude,
the key that opens the lock of angelic realities.
The mind of the desireless desire is empowered in its state of
Harmony
which keeps rising in the essence of gratitude,
and serves to inspire
even as gratitude enables the flow of receiving grace.
A mind that unlocks this secret is an emperor, whose higher
Consciousness serves humanity in the knowing,
in the desireless desire of the we.
The ancient intent, Siva be
Be the Prophet. Aum Namah Sivaya

The sacred fire alight represents the Divine invoked in ourselves. The very nature of connecting with Source enables us to attain the calm and Peace that begins with letting go of any desire, and to feel gratitude. When we step into the state of mind that is of gratitude and less attachment to any desire, we are aligning our mind to Source, and each thought gains potency. When we step back into the womb of infinity, the meditative mind, we understand and realize the desireless desire.

Manifestation then unfolds in ease with each thought from this conscious mind.

Consciousness Sutra 5. Inner Door of Love

We are the lucky ones who know the inner door to be supreme happiness
even as the mind jumps entwined with the ups and downs of human realities.
The calm beyond human emotions and realities created by the mind
is the vast being who dwells inside as the ocean of love.
Meditate to attain the vast love lit by the luminescent inner lamp.
Each thought bubble from the inner shrine is love.
As love, Siva be.
Be the Prophet. Aum Namah Sivaya

The most precious Grace we can have for ourselves is the meditative state of mind. Human realities come with their ups and downs, but when we are aware of the sacred ocean space of love within, in the meditative state of mind, we are able to perceive everything from the wisdom perspective.
No matter what the ups and downs are, a meditative mind is able to harmonize the way we think and react to circumstances. When each thought arises from this ocean of love within ourselves, we are bringing forth the most beautiful expression of infinity into reality from a mind that has been blessed. Then blessed we are to be in the Grace of a meditative mind.

Consciousness is incubated in meditation.

Consciousness Sutra 6. Union of All Paths

The union with Source with entirety is like
using all five fingers of the hand –
Divine love, bhakti; heart's work; tapas and meditation;
hatha yoga, dance and any activity that surrenders
Source's joyful seekings to be joy.
Undiluted joy grips the five fingers of aspiration to
break free of the mind and past to the freedom to be.
With all paths to Source woven each day as play.
Wellbeing, Abundance, Harmony, love and inspiration is the
wealth of Consciousness, the gift of Source union.
In the Yogic unions, Siva be.
Be the Prophet. Aum Namah Sivaya

Each day is a pilgrimage. When we weave together all that we do in states of joy, surrendered to Source, this is Yoga, the cosmic union through each moment.

In wisdom is the knowing; bhakti as Divine Love; work as in unfolding the highest purpose of our heart; meditation as in being in the core within ourselves as tranquility, Peace and Harmony; and as in Hatha Yoga, tai chi, running, dancing or any other means wherein the body is surrendered to the states of joy in attainment of Source – all the goodness we could wish for as the mind, body and soul happens.

Each pilgrimage to our heart center is Consciousness set alight – this aligns our inner and outer realities whatever we do.

Consciousness Sutra 7. Stillness in Gratitude

Gratitude is the grace of wisdom that awakens the deeper journey.
Gratitude is the pulse of life within the human experience.
Gratitude is the gift of grace for masters
who open the wisdom doors
gratitude is the awareness of oneness,
which leads us to the joys of sitting still within the pulse of life
– to meditate and be.
Gratitude awakens the grace to stillness
that holds the dance of expanding Consciousness.
In gratefulness of being joy, Siva be
Be the Prophet. Aum Namah Sivaya

Yogis sit still for hours, if not for days, or months. Guru Ayya sat still for 18 years meditating! The Grace to be still is most sought after and yet it is not easily attained. Attainment of stillness begins with realizing gratitude as the essence of each thought that kindles the joyous states. We venerate the ones who open our door to Consciousness as the Guru, with expression of gratitude. In the Grace of gratitude, we are able to enjoy the joyous states of the mantra to attain stillness.
The Yogis call the joyous states of bliss and euphoria as 'the dance within'. When we are in the state of bliss to be able to enjoy the dance within, we are able to sit still and enjoy the 'I Am' experience of Source.

Consciousness led by gratitude is lit in stillness.

Consciousness Sutra 8. 'I Am' of the Mantra

The nature of mantra chanting is to absorb the mind and gift
the facet of Source
invoked to be.
With each breath's prayer of invoking the Divine matures
through
the dance of joy,
the breathless presence becomes the experience as mother
kundalini.
Becoming the breath beyond breath presence, we are the
dance of joy as form.
The 'I am' state of oneness is the presence of undiluted joy,
the mantra blessings.
Ascend above each breath in the mantra's grace to be.
In being, Siva be.
Be the Prophet
Aum Namah Sivaya

The chant of mantra establishes the single thought chain as a garland of breath.
Through breath and bliss of Source union, we gradually begin to attune to the breathless breath of perpetual joy. The inherent blessing of the mantra awakened by the breathless breath is realization of the invoked Divinity within us – as the 'I Am' experience. The initial sporadic happiness of the 'I Am' experience evolves with our deeper journeys through Consciousness.

Our ability to perceive everything and every moment from the 'All is a part of me; I am a part of it All; I am' now gives way to a thought that is greater than the circumstance and perception and need to dictate how we wish it all to be – instead all is 'As is'. In rising above to the higher realms of the mind, we summon the universe as in each thought in all the goodness and blessings.

The 'I Am' is Consciousness.

Consciousness Sutra 9. Power of Tapas

Descending into our inner fire is our prayer magnified with intent.
With the nurturing of the loud silence,
the inward mind immersed in mantra fire is tapas.
The mantra fire within is nurtured with every breath
as the garland of Divine love.
Impossible impasse situations are resolved as boons through tapas.
Desired realities bloom with focused intent held through tapas.
The intent of desireless desire as that for humanity grows the tapas fire as
the uplifting grand instrument of Source to be.
The fire of grace, the tapas Yogi be.
Be the Prophet. Aum Namah Sivaya

Yogis sit still for hours, if not for days, or months. Guru Ayya sat still for 18 years meditating! The Grace to be still is most sought after and yet it is not easily attained. Attainment of stillness begins with realizing gratitude as the essence of each thought that kindles the joyous states. We venerate the ones who open our door to Consciousness as the Guru, with expression of gratitude. In the Grace of gratitude, we are able to enjoy the joyous states of the mantra to attain stillness.

The Yogis call the joyous states of bliss and euphoria as 'the dance within'. When we are in the state of bliss to be able to enjoy the dance within, we are able to sit still and enjoy the 'I Am' experience of Source.

Consciousness led by gratitude is lit in stillness.

Consciousness Sutra 10. Efficiency of Thought

Consciousness ascends with intensity of single thought focus and Divine grace,
aligning the mind to the eagle's view above human realities.
Burn away karmic baggage to be the lightness
that glides through timelessness.
Each moment becomes efficiency of time that we define in focus,
the knowing and in the effortless grace to glide.
Being the wings of higher Consciousness, unfold realities in ease.
In the knowing, Siva be.
Be the Prophet. Aum Namah Sivaya.

From the foothills, our mind conceives the mountain as huge. Once we climb above to the peak of that mountain, the same mountain now perceives all that is below as beautiful scenery. The beautiful scenery is the realities we perceive with a meditative mind. As we climb above in higher Consciousness to perceive human realities, we see all that life holds for us, as in opportunities, threats, strengths and weaknesses from above, like an eagle. We are able to think outside the limits of the mind for solutions and in creativity. A meditative mind is able to 'see' and in action 'glide' like an eagle. Each thought becomes efficient and we are able work reality with a potent mind.

Climb above to Consciousness to address realities with the knowing.

Consciousness Sutra 11. Flow to be One and Oneness

Scriptures guide the mind to Source as the river to an ocean
with intellect becoming wisdom.
Fluidity and flow is the grace that becomes the ocean of
oneness
and its lack is stagnancy of ignorance.
Flow into being the ocean of oneness devoid of the mind in
humility
from the ocean of oneness, each thought is scripture.
Each breath flowing to be the breathless being, free of
memory and
emotion, gives birth to perfect wisdom.
The expanding journey of being is the sacred flow.
The ocean of wisdom, Siva be.
Be the Prophet. Aum Namah Sivaya

All Prophets and Sages of Consciousness were aligned to Source – they were able to channel from direct experience. Prophet Mohammed and all other Masters of Consciousness flow and are in the flow of Source. The moment we step outside the flow to simply parrot and memorize rigidities of past scriptures, we block the flow of inspiration, love, freedom and joys of being near the Source as Source-connected.
We evolve each step of the way with scriptures initially guiding our intellect. As the doors to Consciousness open, our intellect becomes wisdom and our every thought becomes the scripture.

In the flow of intellect to wisdom, Consciousness is our journey beyond beliefs into the direct experience of cosmic union.

Consciousness Sutra 12. Fierce Grace

Burn our own ego, the Source of emotions, to utilize the fierce facets of the Divine in grace of expanding Consciousness.
Climb above and be the vibrant Harmony where good thoughts emanate –
love, forgiveness, compassion and understanding as goodness.
To utilize the Source to validate anger and subdue enemies is like a policeman stealing.
Goodness is Consciousness.
Goddess kali to protect beings of Consciousness fiercely.
Surrender realities to the goddess within burning our challenges and ego
and her fierce grace of protection is attained.
In goodness of each thought, Siva be.
Be the Prophet. Aum Namah Sivaya

Mother Kali's Grace of destruction of ego awakens the timelessness of wisdom. The Goddess is also depicted as the symbol of Mother Kundalini, the sacred hood of the cobra. For a Yogi, any lower level emotion. from anger to fear, needs be utilized by dissolving it into the sacred Source union fire. The mental state of any emotion is sacrificed into the Goddess for Her to deal with. When we let go of our problems and worries in our surrender, the Goddess then is invoked as a fierce protector of us, as a guide. When we surrender all our lower level emotions to the Goddess, Goddess Kali absorbs it all and takes care of our needs.

Consciousness is always protected by the fierce Grace of the Divine as we thrive to keep it alive with positive energies of the mind.

Consciousness Sutra 13. Awareness of Bliss

Between each thought is a sacred void space that is similar to the void within matter,
and the void that holds all the universes as the thread of Source in its primal vibrancy.
In Yogic union as in the primal vibrancy experienced in bliss of being
the space between thoughts expand and be.
Consciousness is the Divine eternity that produces
sacred thoughts that as wisdom shines.
In the awareness of the primal bliss of no-thought is Consciousness.
In bliss, Siva be.
Be the Prophet. Aum Namah Sivaya

As we journey within through Consciousness, we relate more to infinity as a space within ourselves that has a primal sound as 'AUM'. Beyond the five senses – vision, hearing, smell, touch and taste – is the space of the Spirit – the meditative realm. This meditative realm is in the wedge between thoughts that is experienced as bliss. Upon experiencing this meditative realm, we merge to be the awareness of cosmic union with the infinite sacred space within us and around us. Through intense pilgrimages, chanting mantras and meditation we enhance our awareness of this sacred space of bliss.

This bliss awareness is the subtle shape and form of Consciousness.

Consciousness Sutra 14. Womb in each Breath

In awareness guide breath held to the womb space of the goddess wisdom,
to align the intent of the retention and exhale of breath.
In the retained breath is intent and in the exhale, the journey of surrender
to be the breathless breath of vibrant stillness.
The experience of surrender that absorbs breath in the breath beyond
breath is wisdom of awareness guided by joy, her grace.
In the breath held to be the wisdom that guides, guide each breath to Consciousness.
In the womb of grace, Siva be.
Be the Prophet. Aum Namah Sivaya

Breath guides the way we think. The Yogic wisdom understands breath as the first Guru, the Source of Consciousness. When we are aware of each breath, its inhalation, retention and exhalation, we are able to climb above the mind and seek union with the cosmic womb. We step into the magic of the Now in a moment.

When we utilize breath alongside awareness in the process of reaching the higher conscious state, we step into the threshold of bliss. This bliss within is held to become the bliss of our every reality.

As in bliss we are Consciousness.

Consciousness Sutra 15. Lord Siva, the Destroyer

When each veil of illusion as karma is burnt, layer by layer,
there are still more layers even as there are evolved spirits
that evolve further and further.
Realizing lightness that lights the sacred fires dissolving
each layer of the mind,
we become the center above the mind's rooftop.
The center is the pillar of light that is Source to be.
'The mind' of that beyond the mind is Consciousness of
Siva, the Yogi.
Arising above the sacred ash as past layers adorn the human
as Consciousness.
Dissolved to be, Siva be.
Be the Prophet. Aum Namah Sivaya.

Each layer of thought holds a momentum of the imprinted past that is termed 'karma'. The Yogis invoke Lord Siva as the destroyer of the past, karma and ignorance. Burning away the veil of mind's imprints to transcend into the vast territories of Consciousness, the Spirit is our true being unveiled. Through the journey is the 'I am' experience of all Sages. The spine awakens with the inner fires of meditation to be the pillar of light. With Grace of this invoked presence, our thinking patterns and thought process evolve as layers of the mind's past as imprints is transcended in dissolving ignorance.

The crisp new, free of ignorance, is Consciousness.

Consciousness Sutra 16. Mantra Power

Each mantra is Consciousness imparted by the guru
for each to be the guru.
The potency of the mantra is in the presence of the unbroken lineage of gurus with each
connecting to each in the now within the primal resonance of the mantra.
The vibrant resonance steers though the vast terrains of Consciousness
as guide fulfilling transcendence as grace in awareness.
Lit in the mantra fires,
the mind stills in oneness to the single thought
of the Divine facet so conveyed by the guru.
The mantra vibrations imparts gifts of Consciousness of the guru's living presence.
In the fires of the mantra, Siva be
Be the Prophet. Aum Namah Sivaya

Living in the dense depth of the forest, Siddhar Kakaneswar meditated. As tools of Consciousness he imparted mantras to his disciple Siddhar Rajaswamy. Each mantra contained the Grace to invoke a facet of Divinity and ingrain a dimension of Consciousness. These mantras were then passed to Nandhiji. In the journeys through Consciousness, a single most important tool is the mantra – especially the mantras that come from a Guru lineage. Each mantra is embedded with the Grace of ancient presence and when we recite the mantras we are also invoking all the masters who chanted the mantra previously.

Mantras are able to almost completely transform the mind due to the vibratory transfer of Consciousness; the Sages passed it on so it could reach us in the present day.

Consciousness Sutra 17. Oneness of Consciousness

Being the joys of the wings gliding we are the eagle
that soars to the breathless realm of ever expanding
Consciousness – the mind of the Sages – Turiya.
Ascended in higher Consciousness as in the now,
whirl around the pillar of light with prayers for all of
humanity.
We spin goodness of our blessed joys of ever expanding
Consciousness to be whole,
in prayers for humanity so humanity prays for us.
In prayers for humanity as one, we expand in grace.
In being one, Siva be.
Be the Prophet. Aum Namah Sivaya

One of the perennial teachings of the Siddhars, as directed by Siddhar Rajaswamy, is: intend each prayer for humanity, every living being and for mother Earth.

When we pray as collective oneness of humanity, we allow ourselves to be the instrument of the larger potency of Source energy. The nobility of such intent is also the empowering of Grace of Consciousness for us and every human. In the journey of Consciousness is the dissolving of ego through intent of basic goodness devoid of selfishness.

Consciousness is inclusive of all.

Consciousness Sutra 18. Divine Patience

Be the calm hub of Divine patience within the eye of the hurricane of turbulent realities.
When time is determined from the timelessness of Divine patience,
the inspired flow aligns the hurricane of realities to the calm Harmony of each thought as heart's desires.
We ride the waves of time being the ocean of timelessness.
In Consciousness is Divine patience and the knowing of doings.
In calmness of Harmony, Siva be.
Be the Prophet. Aum Namah Sivaya

At all times, our awareness needs to be an epicenter of calm tranquility within the self. As we become the epicenter, Divine patience and the wisdom of the Now arise; and from that, action can take place immediately. When we are in this calm center, we never react by way of emotions that can trigger wrong thoughts and faulty decision-making. We are able to summon potent thoughts from the calm within to address the turbulence of external realities. The more calm there is within, the greater is our ability to deal with and transform our external realities, no matter how turbulent those realities are.

In the core within is the calm of Consciousness.

Consciousness Sutra 19. Daily Climb

In certainty is the daily inner journey to arise in Consciousness
the discipline that sets us free.
In this climb is the unlearning and surrender of thoughts to the fire within
which eagerly consumes limits of the past to gift the vast now of limitless grace.
The discipline of reigning the mind
through breath to be the breathless joy of Harmony is Yogic grace.
In arising grace, Siva be.
Be the Prophet. Aum Namah Sivaya

Image: Photo of Nandhiji on the peak of Thiruvannamalai mountain in prayers of being One with the five elements – earth, fluid, fire, air and space.

Each day has a gift of joy, to be unlocked, like a pilgrimage above our mind, a daily climb of discipline to free ourselves. In climbing up to attain a higher layer of Consciousness by uniting Source to our mind, we are the Yogi. This climb above is a discipline that can happen exclusively through the joy states we wish for each day – so the 'discipline' is more of a play than an effort, as we unravel our truest nature of the now. The state of Harmony within, as above the mind, is freedom.

Each day's Yogic effort becomes an unyielding discipline that sets us free.

Consciousness Sutra 20. Turiya

When realities weigh heavy entangling the mind,
burst the bubble of time and limits to accomplish
superhuman tasks
through the precious grace of Turiya.
Climb above the mind's rooftop to compress and expand
time from
the peak's vision to map reality desired into manifestations.
In states of Turiya we converge the spirit's knowing with our
innate talent,
desire and passion as the inspired.
In Turiya, Siva be.
Be the Prophet. Aum Namah Sivaya

For Nandhiji, this painting represents the state of Turiya, the super conscious state of the mind of a Yogi – expressed in the energy color theme and in understanding the Spirit that we truly are, the soul awake. Sages call Turiya the sleepless-sleep where time can be warped. When we are inspired, in joy and in the bliss of a meditative mind, we are in the state of Turiya. It is from this state that Mahatma Gandhi and scores of other masters of Consciousness created realities of immenseness for humanity. With daily Yogic practice, the state of Turiya is attained in a natural way as the mind's rooftop holds the super conscious state where each thought is a mighty seed of reality capable of potent manifesting.

The realm of Turiya is Consciousness.

Consciousness Sutra 21. Yogic Mind

The vastness of the blue infinite sky
is the Yogic mind of Grace.
Each thought is cloud-like, moving gently
beneath the sky of awareness.
The shine of the Source as the sun and the glow of the mind
as the moon,
is held by the wholeness of the Yogi
in awareness through the vast space of being.
Breath is the dutiful slave and breath beyond breath, the
master.
Aware we know the sacred purpose within each blessed
breath.
In knowing, Siva be.
Be the Prophet. Aum Namah Sivaya

Understanding the Yogic mind can be done exclusively by experiencing the sublime state of vastness. As we desire to attain the Yogic meditative mind, gradually we are guided to this pristine mind as naturally as a river flowing to the ocean. Attaining this conscious state of mind, we realize the entire universe within ourselves.

Great scientists of India's past were all Yogis who managed to convey great discoveries and inventions that today's science affirms. For example, Carl Sagan confirms the Yogic dating of the birth of planet Earth in total accord with today's scientific calculations. This was due to the ability of the Yogi to see the oneness beyond the mind and conceptualize this wisdom as intellect. This Yogic mind gave birth to astronomy, ayurveda, mathematics etc. The attainment of a Yogic mind is today easily accessible by anyone through tools of Consciousness.

Utilizing the Yogic tools expand Consciousness as a Yogi.

Consciousness Sutra 22. Tantiram Of Merging

Merge time, space and matter through which all realities are perceived
and align realities and Source wisdom.
Uniting awareness of timelessness with time,
infinite of space and the five elements,
attain the sacred tantric wisdom.
Ignite fire of joy that converges the cosmic Divine with sacred realities.
In tantiram is the wisdom of joy in the union of infinity with finite.
In joys of the sacred unions, Siva be.
Be the Prophet. Aum Namah Sivaya

The Siddhar's teachings are called 'Tantiram', the roots of tantra. In this teaching of tantiram is the merging of the infinite with the finite as through states of joy, with joy in itself the seeds of wisdom. As we journey through Consciousness, we seek to unite the colossal cosmic infinity with the finite of human realities and in this union is the vibrancy of joy. This vibrancy of joy is the primal dance that stills the mind while expanding Consciousness to realize the wisdom of oneness. In the tantric experience of oneness, intellect shines as in the genius of our each thought and action.

In realizing joys of cosmic union, Consciousness awakens.

Consciousness Sutra 23. Perfect Each Thought

In seeking thoughts perfectly aligned with Source
is the need to climb above to be the vastness of the sky,
in Harmony, in love, as freedom, bliss –
In expanding joyful Consciousness states of Turiya
each thought transforms karma to dharma in Divine grace.
Each thought flows from the inspired knowing to be the
magic of reality.
perfect intellect is the offspring of the blessed mind.
In wisdom of being, Siva be.
Be the Prophet. Aum Namah Sivaya

In the Siddhar pathway is direct experience devoid of beliefs. Lord Brahma, the creator, represents our ego, bringing us the realities we face, and creating realities from each thought. Lord Vishnu, the sustainer, is our awareness – the Source-connected mind that takes care of us. Lord Siva is our soul that in realization is the Spirit/Holy Ghost. When we are aware of each thought springing from our mind, we are able to steer each thought to perfection as the essentials of Consciousness.

Aware of the mind of Consciousness, each thought arising consumes our past, and our karma, to become Grace, the dharma.

Consciousness Sutra 24. Power to Manifest

Empowering the Yogic mind,
dharma of doing creates magnificent realities.
The steadfast passion of intent to manifest
and the singular focus in the inspiration in doings become entwined.
The Yogi withstands the ups and downs of reality with joyful ease.
In the ocean of the knowing resides persistency
that determines each thought to grandness of realities.
In the depth behind thought, Siva be.
Be the Prophet. Aum Namah Sivaya

The Yogic life, especially when in the human world, maintains a constant bridge between the left brain of practical, rational thinking and the right brain meditative cosmic mind. A Yogi develops inherent skills of enhanced focus through training the mind to meditate. The Yogi utilizes this mind to further levels of Consciousness by summoning and invoking the Divine through meditation, through puja (rituals); through the fire and all other tools of Consciousness. When confronting realities and when wanting to manifest, a Yogi achieves effectiveness in accomplishing due to the mind that is trained in persistency of focus supported by waves of intense inspiration.

Enhancing Consciousness, summon each desire to be reality.

Consciousness Sutra 25. Enlightened Vortex

To be in the vortex of Source union is enlightenment –
space of overflowing joy merged in the Divine.
Awareness beyond thought in the womb of no-thought,
and in the joys of the Divine is this vortex of being light.
In our caves of depth within of each breath's moment
is the sacred vortex of enlightened grace –
Consciousness.
Awake, Siva be.
Be the Prophet. Aum Namah Sivaya

In the moment of Divine union, we are enlightened. Yogis are able to expand this state of mind for all times. Masters like Amma are not only in the perpetual Divine love state but also are able to function in daily realities alongside a cosmic mind. When we are in this vortex of enlightenment, we are protected, guided and blessed each moment. The moments after experiencing this Source union joy, the vortex of enlightenment, our mind is effortlessly in meditation for extended periods of time. When we comprehend our daily rituals of bhakti, Divine love as a key to enlightenment and the meditative mind created by joys and ecstasy of Source union, we enhance our Consciousness.

Bhakti is Consciousness that gifts the meditative state of mind with ease.

Consciousness Sutra 26. Evolve humanity

Each thought wave ripples vibrating essence of joy from within.
Below is the ocean of depth in its wisdom of silence of being whole.
Below is the knowing of that beyond death.
Above is the awareness of being the spirit, the 'We'.
With awareness of being the cosmic being,
each thought vibrates as Source power for humanity's evolution of Consciousness.
As oneness that evolves, Siva be.
Be the Prophet. Aum Namah Sivaya.

To a realized master, death and rebirth is in every breath. Death is that of body Consciousness, ego and limits of the mind. Rebirth is that of the cosmic mind of being the Spirit. In this realization is liberation. When awake as in liberated, each prayer and each moment of meditation is for humanity as there is no more individual ego or identity left.

Such realized masters continually gift humanity with the Grace of higher Consciousness – so that each of us attain our fullest potential in goodness.

Consciousness Sutra 27. Awaken to be the Angel

Awake to be the vastness of spirit,
the eternal now moment aligns with the kundalini fire of
Divine presence.
Lit within as the devotional lamp we light outside, we
awaken to be the
eternal presence.
Evolution of millions of years towards becoming human
now transforms us to becoming angelic in a moment –
With the intent of ancient oneness to represent the knowing
and the purpose.
The angelic awake, Siva be.
Be the Prophet. Aum Namah Sivaya

By lighting a lamp to invoke the Divine, we are lighting an inner fire within ourselves as Mother Kundalini. Our odyssey to the Divine evolves us exponentially. When we awaken to Consciousness, we evolve. Millions of years of human progress become transformed into mere days, months and years within our lifetime to become Angelic. A higher conscious master is an Angel in the body.

For a master of higher Consciousness, the reality is always heaven, no matter what the situation is. For an Angelic Being, each thought is pure mastery of the limited that mobilizes the realms of Source into human realities. Light a lamp to Source to connect each day.

Grow Consciousness by lighting the inner fire.

Consciousness Sutra 28. Eternity of Each Breath

In the beginning and in the end,
as that before birth and after death is the vibrancy of the eternal,
and in the middle, is the karmic identity we take as human with counted breaths.
In uniting the eternal and the temporary,
we create the reality of paradise in the liberated knowing our truth of eternal being.
Liberated in unlearning to realize the eternity within each breath, we are Consciousness.
Knowing the breath beyond breath as breath, Siva be.
Be the Prophet. Aum Namah Sivaya

In the sojourn into ourselves to know death and birth as just a flash of time like the flicker of our eyelids, we realize the eternal being we truly are. The worship of Lord Siva as in the form of a Lingam helps conceive Consciousness, as the Lingam represents the form of infinity. It is our mind and ego that confines us to our identity of 'me', 'mine' and 'I'. When we unlearn through the Grace of our connection with Source, we align to being Lord Siva, the eternal being – the Spirit.

The effective way to enhance our meditation is to aggregate the 'I am' experience of Lord Siva through dissolving each thought that reveals the truth of who we are– Lord Siva, the Supreme Self.

In unlearning from the mind clutter and ignorance of identity, we awaken to Consciousness.

Consciousness Sutra 29. Be the Scriptures

The flow of wisdom from the bliss of Divine union creates
scriptures of life that blossoms and
as each potent thought.
All Prophets agree to scriptures before them but none
followed them blindly.
The now moment of Consciousness holds truth beyond all
scriptures of the past dictating perfect wisdom in the now.
From the joys of Consciousness, each thought is the
liberating scripture.
In freedom of attaining Source wisdom, Siva be.
Be the Prophet. Aum Namah Sivaya

All scriptures hold the truth of the sacred moment in time experienced by all Prophets and Sages of the past. These scriptures are valuable for guiding each of us to the core goodness of being human. The truth each of these realized masters expressed is the same truth that any realized being at any time in the past or future will experience. But each experience with Source union is unique to each person. When we awaken to the reality of our own beingness, each thought is a scripture.

Consciousness attained in the Now is truth behind all scriptures.

Consciousness Sutra 30. Magic of Now

In stillness sustained we grow the seeds of intent
incubating the now to its magical reality.
Boredom to excitement.
Thoughts whirl to singular focus.
The blessings of the void-mind is the sacred flow
that is causal of the magic in the now.
In Turiya is the 'flow' is the cosmic union
fulfilling each breath's intent
time dissolves to timelessness of the spirit realm in the flow.
In Turiya, Siva be.
Be the Prophet. Aum Namah Sivaya

When we meditate to expand our Consciousness, we perceive reality from an evolved perspective. The Yogic mindset is able to create the miraculous magic of each moment at all times. Even when doing mundane chores, a Yogi is able to tap into the flow of inspiration. Holding unwavering focus, the mind of Consciousness is efficient and effective in dealing with every day realities by being. The vast void mind of awareness is aligned to the world of all enlightened beings of the past as in the moment of now – alight as a Lamp.

The magic of Now is Consciousness.

Consciousness Sutra 31. Goddess Grace

The grace of the goddess is the 'flow'
arising from the breathless breath to breath through
the resonant consuming joys of bhakti fire.
In the grace of the ascending fire she is the evolving energies
of Consciousness awakening and arising.
Awakening lord Siva in her entwined joy,
she is primal heart wisdom of spirit and the empowered
intellect.
In joys of kundalini's dance, Siva be.
Be the Prophet. Aum Namah Sivaya

The joyous states of Source union within ourselves is Goddess Kundalini. This inner fire activates our awareness of being the Spirit, Lord Siva. This union is activated by Divine love, bhakti. Mother Kundalini, our inner fire, is depicted in Western and Eastern traditions as the halo drawn around saints and realized masters. Praying, contemplating, meditating, chanting, dancing, Yoga and any activity uniting us to Source awakens our inner fire, Goddess Kundalini. Joy is the path to the Divine and in this joy is the bridge between cosmic wisdom and sharpened intellect converging together to be the 'flow'. In this flow moment is the vortex of mastery of the situation and mastery of doings as genius.

Consciousness is the Grace of the Goddess.

Consciousness Sutra 32. wisdom Beyond Death

Emerging as Consciousness, we are witness
to our death and rebirth in each moment,
expanding expanded in being.
Death is losing of the past mind imprints to evolve to next
state of Consciousness
imparting the greatest of all teaching
is the wisdom of death that conveys the wisdom of rebirth.
Awake realizing the wisdom of death,
each moment of eternal is life celebrated in being.
As deathless Siva be.
Be the Prophet. Aum Namah Sivaya

It is a universal experience of nearly all humans to speak of the 'heavens' in the near death experience. The most profound wisdom is attained when we go through a near death experience. The zeal and enthusiasm to seek the Divine after a near death experience or the 'born again' experience comes from understanding death itself as the teacher. For a Yogi, each moment contains the experience of death as in surrender of the mind and the past that yields to awakening to the wisdom of Spirit as an eternal being in the human body. Having understood the Yogic truth, not a moment in life is wasted.

Life unfolded attaining Consciousness is celebrations and the intent to have more of Consciousness.

Consciousness Sutra 33. Ocean of Bliss

Beneath the ripples of joy is
the ocean of bliss.
In vibrant stillness of bliss hold each moment in
timelessness to swim in Source grace, awake.
Thoughts perceived from this sacred Harmony define time
and
realities that fulfill to inspire.
The magic of timelessness springs from roots of
Consciousness
in the duty to be ocean of bliss – to define time.
In bliss grace, Siva be.
Be the Prophet. Aum Namah Sivaya

Creating the foundation of Consciousness behind every thought as an ocean of bliss, we are in the receiving end of Grace. Divine joys enhance more of joyful realities. The key to attain the state of timelessness and ignite Consciousness is in developing a meditative mind. This meditative mind is roused through understanding that this is our intrinsic inherent birth right. We tune into this mind through assuming our primal being of bliss. We realize that our experiences of time needs to come from the state of bliss at all times.

Bliss is Consciousness. Consciousness grows Consciousness as bliss creating wisdom.

Consciousness Sutra 34. We the Angelic

When the monkey of 'i' and 'mine' of ego are scorched in the fire of cosmic union,
the radiant mind of Harmony emerges to transcend the human to be angelic.
In this fire of evolution are the joys of focus
that awaken the genius with special powers of Consciousness magnified
by the angelic 'we' of oneness.
The 'we' of Consciousness dissolves the 'I' of limits
The limitless, Siva be.
Be the Prophet. Aum Namah Sivaya

Our evolution from animal tendencies of the human to become the Angelic being is in the destruction of our ego and the self-limiting identity of 'me' and 'I'. With the burning away of ignorance that is contained by our ego, our shining bright Consciousness is revealed. With awareness of ourselves no more contained as in the limits of ego, we become one with angelic collectiveness as the 'We'. The angelic true identity of ours is super humanly capable of amazing doings inspired by geniuses.

The Grace of Consciousness is fulfillment and inspiration transcending limits of circumstance.

Consciousness Sutra 35. Magnificence of the Vision

The Grace of a magnificent vision gifts
inspired baby steps of each day
with focus that converges time, space and matter.
The inner wheel of grace moves with
Dharma of action unveiling the vision of purpose in our doings.
Grace flows in blessings of inspiration, wellbeing and the knowing with
highest human purpose unveiled.
Within and beyond is an ancient intent in purpose and the vision's inspiring grace.
In humanity's ascendance grace, Siva be.
Be the Prophet. Aum Namah Sivaya

When we unravel the awakened state of the mind as a journey through Consciousness, we understand our highest purpose as a vision. We come to know the intention for us in this body and time. With Yogic focus and Grace we set about creating the realities to manifest our heart's intent. Our work becomes dharma, the heart's duty. The universe works alongside us to fulfill this intent. This intent of highest purpose is the collective intent of all conscious masters before us.

Awakening to our highest vision, our heart's work begins with a power of Consciousness unraveling the dream to reality.

Consciousness Sutra 36. Key to Consciousness

Mantras gifts of our gurus converge our mind to the single pointedness
thought – the key to the journey beyond the mind.
The ancient primal thread of vibrant wisdom presence of the gurus
become one in the expanding single thought.
The mantra fire invokes the ancient presence of the lineage of gurus.
In grace of all gurus through the mantra blessings evolve.
As mantra blessings, Siva be.
Be the Prophet. Aum Namah Sivaya

Most of India's known mantras are from the traditional vedic branch where there is much of intellect to be utilized in memorizing it. The Siddhar mantras are shockingly simple – sometimes as simple as 'Siva Sivaa'. Each mantra contains a mountain of energy to tap into. To make the mantra even more powerful in its potency, the Siddhar Sages step into the 'I am' awareness of the invoked Divinity within the mantra. The mantras are powerful as they convey the wisdom vibrations of all the Gurus before as our own Consciousness.

Mantras are seeds to Consciousness passed as blessings of the Guru to awaken our inner Guru.

Consciousness Sutra 37. Our First Gurus

The guru is Consciousness and our first guru is our father and mother.
Rub our palms together with gratitude and love –
Thinking of our mother as the left palm and father as the right palm, our first gurus.
Creating gentle warmth and placing your palms over your closed eyes,
receive the blessings of love, caring, health and Divine grace.
Each cell in the body responds in gratitude in acknowledgement
to blessings of our parents, our creators.
Each awake cell stimulates the mind in its awakening.
In grace of origin, Siva be.
Be the Prophet. Aum Namah Sivaya

Siddhar Sages teach that through honoring, caring and worshiping of our parents we gain huge blessings. Parents are our first Gurus. When we honor our Guru, the one who paved our way to higher Consciousness, we are aligned to the Grace that enhances our journey even further. The Grace of the Guru as the inner guide is important. The first Gurus are our Mothers and Fathers. On the lap of our Mother and Father, we were given our first teachings. When we honor our Mother and Father as our Guru through gratitude, each cell in our body receives the energy of healing and wellbeing. Our subconscious mind awakens. Our mind becomes more receptive to higher positive emotions with the bed of gratitude as energy. Rubbing our palms and thinking of our parents as the first ritual when we wake up enables our thought flow from a higher conscious level. This simple ritual can be done at any time – whenever we desire the blessings of a higher thought or simply a shift to higher energy fields. In expressing gratitude and love to our Mother and Father, we open the doors to the blossoming of our mind.

Consciousness thrives in acknowledgement of gratitude to all our Gurus, our parents being the first of all Gurus.

Consciousness Sutra 38. Sacred Roots

The Divinely aroused roots blaze the past to completion in the now.
Primal patterns of thought imprints of karma are dissolved in the light
of the lord ganesh, the root's grace.
Burning the past of karma and limits is wholeness and ascendance
grace to climb above the navel.
Above the navel is the guru's Grace, the root's arising fires.
The lit roots of Consciousness, Siva be.
Be the Prophet. Aum Namah Sivaya

In the root chakra is the Grace to evolve. When we are complete in the elementary needs by way of responsibility and fulfillment, we climb above to the next layer of Consciousness. It is in the ability to dissolve the past of all its darkness into light as to forgive and to be forgiven that we are able to move on with lightness. Lord Ganesh awakens us to the Now that is able to work with millions of years of our past in evolution and transform us to the highest aspiration of being human – to evolve to be the Guru, as Consciousness.

Consciousness Sutra 39. Goddess of Joy!

The mantra's potency is in the awakening ancient heart song of each.
The baptism of the now is in the joyful presence of the lit goddess.
The heart's song's fluidity of the goddess grace is the primal fire.
The flowing Consciousness is rapture of joy, the supreme grace of Divine love
our realties blossom flowing as joys of the heart, lit by the heart song.
In the sacredness of joy, Siva be.
Be the Prophet. Aum Namah Sivaya

From all of history, children in all cultures imbibe nursery rhymes as they kindle a state of joy. The kindling of the heart song by the mantra is like an ancient fire lit – an initiation by itself. Every mantra has within it a component of igniting the heart song or being the heart song itself. The heart song is the Goddess, is fluid and able to hold our realities perceived in fluidity. When realities are perceived as natural dynamic changes containing both good and bad qualities, through the Grace of our heart song we attain the 'flow' of Consciousness. The flow of Consciousness, being in states of joy and bliss through the thought process, is blessings of the Goddess within.

Receiving a mantra is baptism. Awakening the heart song by way of the mantra, Consciousness is ignited.

Consciousness Sutra 40. Mother Kundalini's Ascent

Attainment of Yogic union in each state of Consciousness
is the wisdom of wholeness in the form of
Mother Kundalini's sparkling ascent.
From an ascetic of poverty Consciousness seeking
transformation to be the Sage is the arising mother
kundalini and her grace.
As she arises, realities blossom.
In Mother Kundalini's rise of expanding Consciousness is
our evolution
from human to angelic.
The awake fire, Siva be.
Be the Prophet. Aum Namah Sivaya

Each chakra holds a layer of transformational wisdom of Consciousness when Mother Kundalini arises. For example: the root chakra transforms the primal instincts to that of higher wisdom; the navel chakra awakens the inner Guru wisdom; the solar plexus chakra awakens our super-normal abilities, the Siddhis etc. Each layer of Consciousness ripens with the ascent of Mother Kundalini. Evolution of a seeker to a realized Sage, attaining mastery of Consciousness, would have transformed realities on several layers.

When whole in attainment of knowing, Consciousness completes us as we become the emperor.

Consciousness Sutra 41. Sacred Fires of Union

The fire within grows the roots of Consciousness
for the seedling to evolve to be the tree.
The fire within is wisdom and inspiration that guides.
the fire within is grace that heals and protects.
In Yogic union, grace flows from the fires of Source union.
Lit within is grace of several life times attained.
Awake in the sacred inner fire tended is mastery of
Consciousness and realities.
In grace light, Siva be.
Be the Prophet. Aum Namah Sivaya

In recent history, the author of the book *Autobiography of a Yogi*, Yogi Sri Paramahamsa Yogananda, talked about the inner fire of a Yogi through all his teachings. He reminded us of the Yogic rule to not burn a Yogi, as the body was constantly consumed by an inner fire to acquire vibrancy of eternity. This truth became self-evident in 1952 in Los Angeles, when Sri Paramahamsa left his body. His body showed no signs of decay for over 20 days. A notarized statement signed by the Director of Forest Lawn Memorial-Park testified: 'No physical disintegration was visible in his body even twenty days after death...This state of perfect preservation of a body is, so far as we know from mortuary annals, an unparalleled one. Yogananda's body was apparently in a phenomenal state of immutability.'

Consciousness is the inner lamp lit as awareness beneath each breath and each thought.

Consciousness Sutra 42. The New

The first sacred death is the grace of wisdom
to let go of past, beliefs and conditioning.
The dead past as ash is sacred awareness to
move past to the now.
Above the mind is the blessing of Consciousness
with gifts of the crisp new destined for each.
Embracing the now is grace of Consciousness.
In the ash of the past arising as the new, Siva be.
Be the Prophet. Aum Namah Sivaya

To be able to let go of the past, the mind in its momentum of thought imprints and patterns in itself is Grace. Realities often spark the mind into reacting to a thought based on the previous patterns stored; for example, reacting to an insult by way of anger as response. In our daily Yogic journey, we constantly seek the new through letting go and burning away the past imprints of the mind. In the inhalation through the ida, the moon breath, retention through the pingala, the sun breath and exhalation through the susumna, the spine, we evolve through death to new circumstance in its potential, each breath.

The constant growth of Consciousness in part is the ability to embrace change and the new.

Consciousness Sutra 43. Nectar of Transcendence

Nectar of grace flows from the inner song of Source union
in every dimension of reality comprehended.
Each form of Source as such the reality and each reality as such Source.
Nourished in the bliss to primal Harmony is the nectar of Consciousness
in the primal Harmony is the nectar of transcendence.
In primal Harmony, Siva be.
Be the Prophet. Aum Namah Sivaya

In human realities of the ups and downs is the awareness we cultivate that every facet of reality is Source and Source is in every facet of reality. In realizing the play of Source as reality, we attain the primal Harmony of each moment and circumstance. We are gifted with the Divine nectar of Harmony to be aware of this human Dharma and this awareness is the nectar of transcendence. In this primal Harmony is the dance of joy enjoyed by the Yogis at all times and through every circumstance of life.

When each thought aligns to primal Harmony, we are in states of arising Consciousness evolving and transcending each breath.

Consciousness Sutra 44. Break Free of Time

The 24 hour cycle of day and night imprisons the mind to time.
In the 24 hours is the mind in its moods and the day and night.
By lighting the inner lamp at least once a day,
awaken the spirit of being to the essence of timelessness.
When in tune with timelessness expand to be.
In time, celebrate the freedom of timelessness defining time
As in eternal timelessness, Siva be.
Be the Prophet. Aum Namah Sivaya

Each day, we wake up and sleep as dictated by the 24 hour cycle of day and night. Our mind too has its natural ups and downs in its moods. We are prisoners of experienced time and the mind's momentum. When we light a lamp each day to Source connect, we step into the timelessness realm that gradually frees us from our mind and the 24 hour cycle. To connect with Source reveals to us an ultimate truth – that all that we perceive, understand and think comes from the bed of thought- Consciousness and this Consciousness is of timeless reality connected with Source/Infinity/God. In the Yogic journey is the realm of sleepless sleep wherein the 24 hour cycle is broken through attainment of the state of Turiya. Turiya is the state of super Consciousness. This begins with our own inner journey to connect with Source to determine time from our timelessness as Being.

In escaping from the prison of time and the mind, Consciousness dwells.

Consciousness Sutra 45. Inspired Life's Play

In life's purpose unfolded is the grace of 'flow'
that condenses time, space and matter together
in the inspired play, the Divine blessings of Turiya.
As five fingers, each capable of a specific task each,
is the convergence of each circumstance of life's circus.
Be the vortex of the mighty now in joyful mastery of life
attaining the flow.
Mastering life's circus, Siva be.
Be the Prophet. Aum Namah Sivaya

When life's drama as a circus becomes inspired play, we master our circumstances. We attain the sheer Grace of genius the moment we tap into the 'flow'. This flow is a Divine vortex that connects us to Source as a field Consciousness that holds the state of Turiya. When in the state of Turiya, we witness all our past talents, abilities and inspiration come together as the five fingers of each hand. We are the master overseeing the circus of human life in its drama and in our realities. In the vortex of the flow, our heart's intent becomes the realities desired.

In the vortex of the now, attain the 'flow' with Consciousness as blessings.

Consciousness Sutra 46. Heart's Ascendance

In the Yogic journey is the supreme heart center,
the gate to all the heavens above.
Unconditional love awakens the gate of the lotus
blossoms that is pierced by Mother Kundalini.
In the heart's blossom mother kundalini ascends above
to the higher realms above, the realms of Turiya
Be love to conquer mother kundalini's grace.
In heart's grace awake, Siva be.
Be the Prophet. Aum Namah Sivaya

In human realities there are always conditions in love. This conditional love, though better that no love at all, needs to evolve to be love that is unconditional. The heart chakra is the single most important center since it is here that we are able to evolve in love. When we evolve in love, when we realize love as unconditional, we radiate goodness and divinity. It is solely from the heart chakra opening as love that we can progress further to the higher layers of Consciousness that reside in the higher chakras – the throat, the crown and third eye chakra centers. Often it is the heart chakra opening that is most challenging and when mastered, the Grace of ascendance pours on us.

As in the awake heart of love is Consciousness.

Consciousness Sutra 47. Journey above in Stillness

Awakening to the expanding oneness
comes the knowing of each layer of the mind
and its rooftop above, beyond the knowing.
Below in the vibrant stillness in ascendance piercing each layer of
mind journeying above to the rooftop and beyond.
Above is the breathless being expanding in surrender and receiving to be.
Each single breath holds the blessings to ascend and be
In wholeness expanding, Siva be.
Be the Prophet. Aum Namah Sivaya

When we are ignited in the first of experiencing Source as bliss, we also understand our mind, thoughts, breath and the journey through breath beyond to the infinity of Source. In this journey is understanding stillness and silence to transcend all the many layers and facets of our mind in its thinking process to climb above to the mind's rooftop.

Once above at the 'rooftop' we understand ourselves as whole, complete and in a perpetual meditative state of Consciousness.

Consciousness Sutra 48. Grace of Yogic Focus

The power of mind to generate realities of each thought
is in convergence of the trinity's grace.
The awakened mind of knowing is lord vishnu.
Awake in being the spirit, lord Siva is worshiped.
Inner fires of passion, inspiration and joy is blessings of the goddess.
Utilize this precious human birth to evolve each breath
converging the trinity –
Lord Vishnu, Lord Siva and Goddess Sakti
in union of the three, Siva be
Be the Prophet. Aum Namah Sivaya

The trinity within the meditative realms comes in the uniting of awareness as the mind (Lord Vishnu); the Spirit (Lord Siva); and the inner fires of Mother Kundalini (Goddess Sakti). Uniting the three Divine facets through our worship and contemplation constitute a potent ritual to enhance the meditative state of the mind.

When we wake up Mother Kundalini through our passionate devotion, we awaken ourselves to be the Spirit, Lord Siva. Our awakened mind that celebrates the sacred joys of worship/ union is Lord Vishnu, awareness.

In understanding the mind, the Spirit and the inner fire as the sacred trinity, Consciousness is enhanced.

Consciousness Sutra 49. Death and Growth

For Consciousness to expand, as the rose plant pruned
the destruction of 'me' 'mine' and 'i' of ego enables
newer realities attuned to heart's joy to sprout.
Source aligned realities inspire ever expanding
Consciousness
with the wisdom of knowing death,
the rebirth in each breath, and
the fire of the awake spirit
that rejuvenates the new of the now.
In grace of realization to surrender and receive, is
Consciousness.
Expanding Consciousness, Siva be.
Be the Prophet. Aum Namah Sivaya

To understand failure and letting go of the past is about understanding the space needed to create the new. In the sacred energies invoked through our inner fire, the newer realities we usher are sustained and nourished.

The pain of letting go of the hurt of the past and ushering in the new is much like a death and rebirth so that Consciousness can flourish.

Consciousness Sutra 50. Tears of Gratitude

The most powerful human expression is tears of gratitude.
Deep from the well of the human essence, tears of the heart spring.
may our supreme prayer each moment be that of gratitude – heartfelt to be expressed as tears of gratitude.
All the blessings counted. all the past the blessings. this moment blessed.
Tears of gratitude in the awe of being whole is grace of the heart goddess.
Goddess laxmi's grace of abundance is gratitude's blessings.
Each moment in expression of gratitude,
Source flows as Consciousness.
In heart's grace to receive, Siva be.
Be the Prophet. Aum Namah Sivaya

Gratitude is an accompaniment of wisdom. Ask any realized being, 'How are you?' and response will be to the effect – 'Grateful' expressed in many ways. When we hold the basic mode of our mind in awe and positivity of our realities through gratitude, the sacred universe allows us to have more of what we truly desire and what is good for ourselves.

An exercise: Rub both your palms together slowly and gently with the intent, 'I am grateful for all that I am, for all that I have, for all my past, for all the present and for all the future.' Place your warm palms over your eyes and receive the blessings of your higher self.

In gratitude for the moment, we are the blessings of Consciousness.

Consciousness Sutra 51. Inner Fire to Be Angelic

Merging the subconscious and awareness
with the super-Consciousness of bliss
through 'tapas',
tend the igniting inner fire.
Devotion, Surrender and Focus become one.
Each thought consumed by the mantra fire awakens the
ocean of bliss
the blessed mind in grace of Harmony
transforms the human to be angelic.
The angelic being, Siva be.
Be the Prophet. Aum Namah Sivaya

The dynamism of Consciousness is in bringing more and more focus as one thought. The Sages of the East have utilized mantras to find the single focus of the mind that ignites the 'inner fire' that is called Tapas. When the inner fire is awake, we step into timelessness that consumes the subconscious mind and the mind of awareness alongside the vaster super-conscious mind of Turiya. When one single thought is held for extended minutes, or hours, or days, or sometimes months and years as Tapas, Consciousness multiplies itself, potent and capable of igniting others to Consciousness.

Tapas becomes a daily discipline of the masters as a mighty tool of Consciousness that generates more and more of Consciousness as a sacred incubation.

Consciousness Sutra 52. Grandness within The Fire

The power of tapas is the empowerment of the now.
When the mind is condensed to single focus
converging grace light,
human realities and ancient intent
merge in Consciousness attained.
Each reality blossoms in the ascending kundalini fire.
The inner fire of timelessness consumes time.
Divine love, bhakti fire is wisdom to have more of Divine love.
Consciousness grows more Consciousness.
In the grace of the inner fires, Siva be.
Be the Prophet. Aum Namah Sivaya

We understand this Source union as Divine Love, or bhakti – and the more of bhakti we experience, we are gifted with more of wisdom. In the attainment of Consciousness is the realization that more Consciousness can be attained through the inner fire of Tapas. As the inner fire is tended and grown through Tapas, we are lifted to higher and higher levels with each level higher acting as an initiation. The first initiation is that of the mundane mind to that of a wisdom mind. Through Tapas of Yoga, the body transforms. Likewise comes a series of evolutions that happen when the inner fires alight.

Within the inner fire of Tapas is Grace of Consciousness.

Consciousness Sutra 53. Leader of Leaders

As the leader of leaders, fearless of death and
knowing our deathless being in each breath,
we are wholeness representing ancient purpose of wholeness.
Blessed in Consciousness, leadership is natural in its
radiance of wisdom.
We utilize 'I' to navigate through joys of doing, serving
humanity and mother earth – while in the humility being the
messenger and tool of ancient intent.
Being light of wholeness, we lead wholeness and the
incomplete.
As leader of the pathway, Siva be.
Be the Prophet. Aum Namah Sivaya

In every part of the world, a conscious being is either a leader leading or sometimes persecuted by the ignorant. Beings of Consciousness make natural leaders as their very aura is radiant and they are charismatic. Consciousness awakens the wholeness in ourselves that takes up the leadership role as heart's purpose and the rest of the society follows with love and admiration. Wholeness is always followed by the incomplete. Wholeness and wholeness respect each other. The whole world gravitates to Consciousness.

Consciousness is leadership.

Consciousness Sutra 54. Awaken the Genius

The blessings of genius in realities
is the intellect and the nurturing awake inner fire
awakening the sacred realm of Turiya in the
grace of inspiration, focus and passion.
The ancient inner fire burning away the 'I'
and the limiting karma is the limitless now of possibilities.
Causal of vast goodness, we are liberated in the grace of
inspiration
that awakens the genius of our doings in the immenseness of
being.
In genius of being, Siva be.
Be the Prophet. Aum Namah Sivaya

When we wake up to higher Consciousness, we grasp the truth of existence, that it is about knowing the law of karma and dharma. We will utilize each of our moments to do our heart's work as dharma. When we do our heart's work, we are gifted by genius in our doings as in the waves of powerful inspiration. In our doings comes inspiration and Grace to evolve and perfect ourselves, as human transforming to be angelic, and all that we do has a sense of perfection to it.

Consciousness awakens the unique genius within each of us.

Consciousness Sutra 55. Selfless Doings

As the supreme Yogi,
empower the mind to be the eagle that glides.
When the heavy mind gets caught up in the karma's net,
it's time to set the mind ablaze in grace.
Through grace of the inner fire,
the lit mind becomes an efficient
vehicle that glides effortlessly
in inspired doings.
In selfless doing is grace that frees us to be.
In Dharma, Siva be.
Be the Prophet. Aum Namah Sivaya

In the inherent nature of our journey, after attaining Consciousness, we still feel caught up by circumstances of limits and turmoil that can be attributed to the karmic past and the collective karma of humanity. The moment we realize this limiting us, we dissolve these limitations by focusing on our heart's work, aligning it to dharma. Dharma is the selfless doings of good, called seva. When we delve into seva as heart's work, all our karmic imprints burn away. Doing dharma burns karma as Grace of the inner fire.

Consciousness is the mind of high vibrancy attained in burning away the emotions and ignorance not desired.

Consciousness Sutra 56. As in Love

To fall in love is to be blessed.
to be in love is blessings.
To be love is to be the blessings.
Expanding love, love becomes more eternal.
Love graduates from its painful nature in attachment to
the joyful overflowing unconditional love.
When intellect surrenders to wisdom, all becomes love.
Through cosmic union be the love form that is the nucleus of
oneness.
Consciousness is love.
As love, Siva be.
Be the Prophet. Aum Namah Sivaya

To fall in love for any reason initiates fires of emotion. When we are in love, we ride on a positive energy compared to not being in love. When we are love, we transcend conditional love to that of the unconditional and we are now flowering in Consciousness. Love is a very important element of Consciousness as it becomes purer with Source union even as our Consciousness is expanded further.

Consciousness is love that is light.

Consciousness Sutra 57. Genius Beyond Mind

Higher Consciousness awakens the unique genius of each,
the 'siddhi'.
all scientists of ancient india were saints.
When awake to step above the mind's rooftop
to be one with the infinite,
we awaken the unique facet of our purpose as human.
The genius wakes up in inspiration, focus and passion.
Each reality then is the masterpiece furthering frontiers of
humanity.
Where inspiration and joyful doings merge, reality expands
from the core of Harmony in the extraordinary magnificence.
In the genius of being, Siva be
Be the Prophet. Aum Namah Sivaya

When we wake up, we are led to the journey of Consciousness that triggers our realization of purpose. It is now that we awaken all the latent powers within ourselves, the 'Siddhis'. Each of us have a unique facet that we alone are the best or extraordinary at and everyone has a unique Siddhi or Siddhis. This Siddhi could be proficiency in mathematics, as an artist, as a politician, or any profession that we deem to be our truest calling. When we follow our heart in the work we do, the super normal abilities as Siddhi kicks in as genius – as the Spirit in perfect alignment with the human. This is depicted as the third eye awakened and the six-pointed star.

Awake in Consciousness and allow your genius to shine.

Consciousness Sutra 58. The Guru

our 'mind' simply reflects thoughts filtered through various conditioning,
which as karma shapes our reality.
in the blessed now, this 'mind' blossoms to realize
the 'mind beyond mind' as the guru beyond the mind.
pure wisdom of guru's grace awakens our awareness of being the limitless.
every thought is scripture emerging from the higher conscious realm, the guru.
this sacred realm is grace of being the river, and the swimmer
and the witness to the river and the swimming.
the guru is all three.
to be grace is to be blessed by Consciousness
that awakens us to be the guru in awareness.
in awareness, Siva be
be the Prophet. Aum Namah Sivaya

As we discard a limited mind and a life of limitation to step into the grandness of vastness, we realize infinity itself to be the Guru and all that we do as Grace. As we traverse through Consciousness that is the Guru, we become the Guru and each thought of ours is perfect in the now, as scriptures.

Consciousness is the Guru, the wisdom.

Consciousness Sutra 59. Dance of wisdom

Realizing Source within all matters and within all the living
is Consciousness.
The dance of infinity within the atom,
The dance of Void, Vastness of space, The dance of Source
in all the living,
In the awareness of the dance of the one
In oneness is Source and wisdom as witness to
the dance of creation, sustenance and destruction.
The vast awake timelessness experiencing time at its the
primal dance.
In the dance of one Siva be.
Be the Prophet.
Aum Namah Sivaya

Consciousness expands our mind to 'See' the oneness within all things. We 'See' through the experiences of joy; through dance. Within this dance is the union of wisdom, Intellect and understanding the oneness of it all. We step into this higher conscious realm of timelessness and experience time knowing the oneness of all that we perceive. In the realm of timelessness holds all possibilities as the power to create, sustain or destroy and each thought arises from this innate potency.

To attain the insight of the perpetual inner 'dance' is what is the mastery of Consciousness.

Consciousness Sutra 60. Consciousness

We are the messengers whose mesSage is
for each to be the messenger,
We are the Source to mantra, tantra and yantra.
Source awareness is in countless forms.
Seeking even greater wholeness in the mantra fires;
in the sacred unions of Source and realities is the tantra;
in the sacred enshrined oneness, our form is the human
yantra.
The mantra, tantra and yantra of Consciousness awakens us
to be.
Our message is oneness of Love that is Ahimsa – seeing
ourselves in each.
our message is the awakening to be one that is many.
the grand oneness awake is one Consciousness, the we
in oneness as one, Siva be.
Be the Prophet. Aum Namah Sivaya

Mantra, tantra and yantra are the three tools to attain Source Consciousness. Mantra is the power within that can evolve; tantra is the union with Source as the physical realities with Source; and yantra is the physical form of Source. When we wake up to be One, we summon the grand immense efficacy of Consciousness to evolve ourselves and humanity. The nature of Consciousness is the realization of being one with its nature- to be compassionate and grasp the wisdom of rejecting violence as the principle of 'Ahimsa'.

Consciousness is the real Peace.

Consciousness Sutra 61. Miracles of Consciousness

The seeds of miracle in manifestation
is in aligning the depth of the subconscious with Source.
the greatest seed of miracle is the love of Source union
which gestates as the inner most desire of Source union –
heart inspired realities desired from Consciousness.
manifesting Source awakens the mind that manifests the now, now.
In the infinite magic of now is the highest aspiration of humans –
to be the Sage of wisdom awaken and knowing purpose
in Source, wisdom, Siva be.
Be the Prophet. Aum Namah Sivaya

In our highest wisdom is the realization to attain more of Consciousness. In this perpetual inner journey through Consciousness, we attain the potency of each thought that serves humanity and is capable of being the miracle of every moment. When our Consciousness becomes potent, we are able to summon the Now we desire, now.

Consciousness is the Lord of Infinity, Lord Siva.

Consciousness Sutra 62. Beingness

In the instinctive deep seeking is the need to connect with others
and in connecting, we experience our realities.
In the even deeper yearning is the need to connect with Source
and in connecting, we experience our truth in beingness.
in connecting to Source we realize ourselves being the billions of light years of timelessness experiencing time in this life.
A whole lifetime in a blink of an eyelid and yet, each moment
the infinity of every breath experience.
Our presence as Consciousness oxygenates planet earth with love, nurturing, fulfillment and inspiration to all, with the inhale of intent.
Each exhaled breath is the sacred flow
in form, time and momentum of tranquility, Peace and Harmony.
We are the form of infinity ascending and expanding with each breath
the infinite enjoying the finite, Siva be
Be the Prophet, Aum Namah Sivaya

Every breath holds our innate need to connect – at first to the realities as in people and circumstances and then to the Source. Through breath to realize our vastness as timeless beings of the infinite, we then perceive the finite as a being of nature of Consciousness.

Being Consciousness, we seek to attain more Consciousness and our every desire manifests as the now, in the instance.

Consciousness Sutra 63. Protective Dolphin Energy

When confronted with shark-like hostile, selfish and ignorant
attitudes of those around us, we swim maintaining the
dolphin-like joy states.
Adorning the resonant shield of inner fire, the power of
tapas,
we are vibrancy of joy form.
The power of tapas spins innermost realities
of Peace, Harmony and Consciousness around the protective
vibrant energies
past karmic patterns are consumed by the triumph of light as
the dolphins over the sharks.
The grace of Source is overwhelmingly protective in its
vibrant presence. Consciousness is the shield of Love,
wisdom and Genius, protected.
In Love as Love, Siva be.
be the Prophet. Aum Namah Sivaya

When we attain Consciousness, we are sometimes seen as weak by the ignorant who sometimes could be predators, shark-like. A shark is an efficient killing machine. When our Consciousness is awake, we know we are protected and guided through life as in Divine patience, as in ability to find solutions beyond the limits of circumstance and as in the energy field of Consciousness. For thousands of years, the Yogis in India roamed in the forests that were also home to robbers, tigers, etc, and they walked sometimes alone, through the length and breadth of India. The Yogis are protected in the vortex of Consciousness.

Consciousness is vibrancy of the Divine that always is victorious.

Consciousness Sutra 64. Preciousness of Each Breath

Our only emotion in the midst of infinite Divine patience
is that of time's apparent waste.
the human body has a shelf life with breath counted for each.
breath holds time and the timelessness
which is witness to human follies and its miracles of thoughts.
as the baby surrendering the mind in breathless joys of Source,
each breath is causal of miracles of reality in the flow
– with not a moment wasted.
Urgency of passion sets priority of that to be done.
Efficiencies of Consciousness are the Divine flow
of focus, passion, priority and inspiration.
In breath's fullness, Siva be.
Be the Prophet. Aum Namah Sivaya

We understand the Yogic term 'Surrender' as an important process of attaining Consciousness. In our daily pursuit of heart's work, we do sometimes feel bogged down by limitations. It is time to step back and surrender all thoughts to attain the Consciousness that holds Divine patience and the instant ability to act in the Now with the wisdom of the Divine 'flow'. In the flow, we summon passion, priority and inspiration and with Yogic focus, the hurdle and obstacles are cleared in our doings.

In Consciousness is the quality of decision to act and manifest.

Consciousness Sutra 65. Root Grace of the Guru

The strong roots awakened by the guru grows deep
to enable the tree of wisdom in its eternal reality to
unfold each breath's knowing.
Lit in the journey, the onslaught and upheavals of karmic
realities
stimulate the inner fire to attain the resilient power of grace.
Our mind is surrendered into the inner fire,
like old leaves withering away so the newer branches sprout,
to bounce back stronger with more mighty thoughts.
The guru in the mantra's presence
is sustaining grace for the roots to grow deeper for the giant
tree of Consciousness.
The roots to all reality, Siva be.
Be the Prophet. Aum Namah Sivaya

The challenges of the world do stimulate our need for a Higher Conscious approach. The Guru is Consciousness and the chanted mantra of a Guru invokes the Guru. We are able to think anew and beyond the limits of realities we perceive when we invoke the Guru's presence as enhanced Consciousness. Life's challenges activate, sustain and nourish our resolve to keep the inner fire lit and growing like the roots. This is the Guru's Grace.

Consciousness is the Guru.

Consciousness Sutra 66. Grace of Resonance

In the secret of the breathless breath
is the sacred resonance space of the eternal spirit,
the guru to thought, Consciousness.
In this ancient resonance is the primal nada,
the dance of the cosmic joy vibrant
as the guru residing
in the mantra fire, bhakti, focus, inspiration, and the inner alight fire.
As energy twirling and spinning, spin resonance to twirl through the spine upwards and
be the awake invoke presence of each breath.
Born again each moment as Consciousness of the invoked through resonance,
tend the inner fires.
As grace of resonance, Siva be.
Be the Prophet. Aum Namah Sivaya

For thousands of years, the sacred wisdom was transferred through the resonance of mantra chants as the most empowered 'Saktipat', the Consciousness awakening energies. To tune into the mantra is to align ourselves into an ancient primordial resonance that vibrates at a high frequency. Our mind and thoughts being frequency, we are in a moment attuned into the vibration of the mantras chanted.

Through breath, with the mantra chants inciting the inner fire of ancient presence, we are the expanding Consciousness.

Consciousness Sutra 67. Six Dimensional

Each thought germinates from its earth-like mother, the mind
and the infinite cosmic Consciousness, its father.
The mind aligns time, matter and space
as a sacred triangle.
Awareness aligns karma, dharma and grace
as a second sacred triangle.
Awake in single focus of Source,
the six-pointed star of the two triangles in union
becomes the third eye awake.
In this sacred union unfold the Divine realities
of being the angelic being.
Transcend converging with the grace of angelic intent
to become the genius of human reality.
We are Consciousness, the birth child of Source.
As the Divine child awakes, Siva be.
Be the Prophet. Aum Namah Sivaya

Tamil is one of the very old languages, as old as Sanskrit, if not older. South India is oldest landmass that had Peace lasting over 3000 years. Surrounded by ocean and a land mass of powerful kingdoms in the north, South India was never invaded from outside. The main deity of worship was Lord Muruga, the Lord of the six-pointed star. The worship of Lord Muruga predates known history. Worshiped as the Guru to Gurus, the Sages acclaim Lord Muruga as in grace of instant transformation. Lord Muruga is a special deity of the Siddhars that awakens us to our truest nature as sons and daughters of the Source- the kernel of meaning within the six-pointed star.

Awakening to the truth of who we are – the Divine Child – we are Consciousness.

Consciousness Sutra 68. Worship of Time

Step into timelessness
and worship timelessness as time,
to define time.
Time is realities of the goddess in form and
timelessness is Source.
Our every thought is magnificent reality when borne of
timelessness
giving birth to the inspired, blessed, abundant, joyful time.
Infinite patience and the action from the now steers
realities with time held in reverence.
Time is a dress chosen to be worn by Consciousness –
blessed by timelessness.
In time as timeless, Siva be.
Be the Prophet. Aum Namah Sivaya

As in realizing timelessness, we have a heightened sense of time. The old Zen adage of 'Chopping wood before awakening and chopping wood after awakening' does not hold true. Once awake, we will want to utilize our time more efficiently by how we act, whether it is in meditation and practices that bring us Harmony or in day-to-day works that has our heart's intent in it. An awakened being, normally, would sooner or later drop out of the rat race of survival mode and instead see each moment of work justifying the highest purpose of existence.

The power of Consciousness creates before us a reality that we desire effortlessly – a conscious being desires only the highest good.

Consciousness Sutra 69. Divine Child Mind

As the mind of a child discards the crying mode
to step into laughter mode in an instant, we steer our mind.
Breaking the karmic patterns by not reacting or
entertaining a thought born of emotions,
we climb above our mind to produce thoughts.
Limitations of realities shrink before the elegance of
Consciousness.
our mind is pure magic when we steer through the mind and
beyond
to ride the Source vehicle of primal Harmony.
Reaping the mind of Source in Consciousness, each moment
is grace of childlike joy.
As the child of Siva, be.
Be the Prophet. Aum Namah Sivaya

We have the choice to utilize a mind that is low in energy, as in emotions that do not serve it, or a mind that is conducive to all positive thoughts. Observing a child to see how quickly the tears and crying can alter to Happiness and Joy, we understand the mind of Consciousness. A mind that is in the vibrancy of Happiness and Positivity nourish the core Harmony that seats Higher Consciousness. The practice of adopting a child-like mind makes the mind a good vehicle to ride on. A child-like mind is blessed to be the wise Divine mind state of Consciousness.

The transformation of the mind to be in Higher Consciousness state could be in an instant.

Consciousness Sutra 70. Daily Ritual

Eating is an important ritual of the physical form.
Source union ritual is important for the life we desire.
Our daily slot of time to be timelessness is worship.
The vibrancy of stillness expands awareness.
The 24 hours of time is but earthly in its sleep, dream and 'awake' states.
Time to surrender. time to dissolve. time to be center as void.
Break free of the cage of time by being, stepping into timelessness.
Through timelessness is the ritual that sets us free to be Consciousness.
Beyond time, beyond the mind, be the timelessness in prayers
all goodness in abundance is the very nature of higher Consciousness.
Source union each day is key to heart dreams aligned realities.
In potency of prayers, Siva as the worshiped be.
Be the Prophet. Aum Namah Sivaya

Each day, celebrate the Source by doing any ritual to enter into Stillness, Timelessness and the Vast Void as a discipline to set ourselves free. Free from the cage that imprisons us to limits we step into super Consciousness that enables every desire and thought as dreams to be true realities. The rituals could be any activity that brings us closer to our heart's joy – Meditation, Yoga, Dancing, Running etc.

Understanding the void mind as the infinity within, grow Consciousness so to be free.

Consciousness Sutra 71. Yogam

Our greatness of being is the blessings of Source union,
Yogam —
who dances as the primal nada within breath,
– who dances as goddess reality unfolded,
– who is lit in the fires of bhakti, Divine love.
– who is Divine love, bhakti, is first treasure of life.
– who has attained the grace of guru
– who leads a life of purpose in Dharma.
loved, abundant, fulfilled, inspired and in the receiving end
of grace, is Yogam
The evolved evolving wholeness, Siva be.
Be the Prophet. Aum Namah Sivaya

Through the Grace of mantra that ignites the primal resonance of inner fire within, our expanding Consciousness brings the awareness of the supreme treasure we carry – Divine love, or Bhakti. With Bhakti, we are blessed with teachers manifested by our seeking. These teachers are the Gurus who expand our awareness of Consciousness through teaching us Dharma. We understand our purpose to be Dharma, the highest heart's purpose of charity, selflessness and caring for others. Consciousness is embedded with the nature of Dharma as it is of the nature of constant expansion through push and pull. The push is our individual effort. The pull is through Grace. To be in Divine Love, to be of wisdom in the knowing and to do work aligned to our heart's dream is Yogam, the richest blessing of Consciousness.

In wholeness of being is Consciousness.

Consciousness Sutra 72. Multiplied Consciousness.

Being eternal and undivided we are the angelic beings.
Experiencing the human
we divide ourselves to many as many as Consciousness multiplied.
When we awaken to be the one as many,
awakening to the intent of this human birth, we are angelic blessings of humanity in uplifting Consciousness.
We are the momentum of the river of love coursing into the ocean of Consciousness grace.
Our own journey and that off humanity's is one.
In ascending Consciousness of humanity, Siva be.
Be the Prophet. Aum Namah Sivaya

In our intent for the welfare of humanity, in prayers and invocations, the more bandwidth of Grace that flows in transforming our own growth. In understanding the oneness of humanity as collective Consciousness as the same as our own, we are able to be the river of love moving all the living towards the ocean of light. In our sojourn within is Consciousness multiplied. We are the Siddhars whose presence amongst humanity ascends each to the angelic by virtue and intensity of intent.

In Consciousness, we are the prayers of humanity.

Consciousness Sutra 73. Yogic Mind

Attaining the Yogic mind that is in ease of effortless
meditation is
our rebirth – each day and each moment
with the foundations of a Harmony within
that allows for continual expansion of the core of Harmony.
From this blessed mind, angelic thoughts are born
Yogic insights from newer threshold of Consciousness is
causal of endless possibilities.
Turiya is Consciousness – the gift to be the angel.
In primal Harmony of Turiya, Siva be.
Be the Prophet. Aum Namah Sivaya

When we drive a wedge within the thought stream momentum to delve into the meditative mind that holds Harmony, we are able to think fresh with thoughts that are. Developing a mind of vaster Consciousness as a Yogi, we possess a super mind that can comprehend beyond the known limits. The key to each perfect thought arising is from growing the Turiya mind state of the Yogi. To attain the Turiya and keep expanding this joyful inspired state is produced through better quality of thoughts. Harmony holds Consciousness.

Consciousness expands from the mind of Harmony.

Consciousness Sutra 74. Our Infinite Being

As one with our father void,
we are the expansive trillions of light years
and still expanding as space and the inner dance.
We are supreme Consciousness.
being the sun beyond the mind; as whole, as expansive,
each thought as planets of reality move around us.
Beyond day and night is Turiya- the bliss of Consciousness.
Each thought from Turiya is infinite becoming the finite,
perfect in form.
As the ancestor of all creations that absorbs to rebirth – each thought, each planet
and each living cell, in joyful grace is the sacred dance of our being.
The dance of the infinite dancer, Siva be.
Be the Prophet. Aum Namah Sivaya

A guidance: Step outside, where you have the sky above you, and raising your hands out, reach out to the infinite saying, 'I am'. In this simple affirmation, allow yourselves to feel the limitless being you are. Bring your hands together, palms together, as in a Namaste. Feel each cell in the body vibrate in infinity. With this simple exercise, sense the euphoria. Hold this euphoria and blissful thought for a moment to understand this feeling as the dance within all things – the sky and each cell in the body. Your Sub-Consciousness remembers this gentle realization of who you truly are. Watch the day unfold as your mind has climbed up higher. The dance within of perpetuity of the infinite is Consciousness. See the entire cosmos within yourselves.

We are limitless Consciousness.

Consciousness Sutra 75. Gratitude

From the womb of void nurturing breath,
each moment is whole in gratitude
for the profoundness of unconditional love realized.
Gratitude paves the way to understand the ever
present Source in each moment.
The mind glides on the wings of joy in lightness in
gratefulness.
Gratitude as first thought nurtures life of wholeness desired.
As whole, Consciousness nurtures more of gratitude as life's
overflowing realities.
In the blossom of life as gratitude, Siva be.
Be the Prophet. Aum Namah Sivaya

The principle within the core of happiness, positivity and a mind nurturing Consciousness is gratitude. When we begin a perception with the feelings of gratitude, all thoughts that follow are tuned to higher frequencies. In the feeling of gratitude is the acknowledgement of the Source and Source's gift of taking care of our every moment – that leads to more of the same. In trying circumstances, when we utilize gratitude as an emotional thought to analyze and think, we are not caught in any lower levels of emotions that carry karmic patterns.

Gratitude brings us into the now.

Consciousness Sutra 76. Dedicated to Navratri: Nine Dimensions of the Goddess.

Infinity is born of the mother, the cosmic womb
in the trinity multiplied within the trinity.
As the bride of the soul imparting wisdom of self-realization
through surrender,
she is the awareness of soul's essence to human purpose.
Her auspicious grace is wisdom of time and timelessness,
in abundant of spiritual and material wealth
and the genius of passion, inspiration
and wellbeing is her grace.
She is victory in human purpose.
fulfilled and inspired to evolve with blessings of the goddess,
celebrate her passionate union in Divine love, bhakti
entwined in the goddess grace, bhakti.
Divine love, Siva be.
Be the Prophet. Aum Namah Sivaya

The Goddess' principle within worship activates the dynamic energies of spiritual endeavor and life realities. Depicted in the yantra as triangles, the Goddess is pure wisdom, abundance in the spiritual and material realities and blessings of the energies that make all things happen. Navratri is dedicated to nine days of Goddess worship – to adore different aspects of the supreme Goddess. On the first three days, the Mother is invoked as a powerful force known as Durga, in order to destroy all our impurities, vices and defects. The next three days, the Mother is adored as a giver of spiritual wealth, Lakshmi, who is considered to have the power of bestowing on her devotees inexhaustible wealth. The final set of three days is spent in worshipping the Mother as the goddess of wisdom, Saraswati. In order to have all-round success in life, we need the blessings of all three aspects of the Divine Mother hence, the worship for nine nights. The worship of the Goddess is the rise of the Divine Feminine of humanity. The feminine symbolizes Consciousness as in compassion, love, understanding, patience and motherhood.

Consciousness is in the ascendance of humanity honoring the feminine.

Consciousness Sutra 77. Inner Music

In the entwining of mind with euphoric joy
is the genius that springs from our heart
singing the most perfect inner 'music'.
The subtle substance of heart's music is.
The poetry of the now, the genius of wisdom
in the joys of mother kundalini is the Turiya state the primal
resonance of joy –
the heart poetry ceaselessly singing.
The singer, the listener and the song are the 'We' of
Consciousness.
In grace of the joyful fires of the goddess.
Siva in the awareness be.
Be the Prophet. Aum Namah Sivaya

To wake up to the 'inner music' is the supreme Grace behind the genius of what we do. This 'music' represents the states of joy that translate to everything that we do – such as the joy of inspiration of an artist, the flow attained by a scientist or the feeling of optimism while taking a walk. Mother Kundalini is the inner fire that initiates primal wisdom of the heart that is perfect as a poetry in reality.

Awakening to Consciousness as the alight heart song; the genius of our doings shine.

Consciousness Sutra 78. Five Elements

Understanding ourselves to be the all, we are aware of our sacredness in each element.
We dissolve into the Divine through each element to be spirit –

through earth, the body; through water, the life force; through fire, intelligence through air, the wisdom; through space, the cosmic oneness.
We attain being one.
The sun, the moon, the stars is within our infinity of being.
Attaining oneness, all the five elements responds to a being of Consciousness.
We are the wisdom within resonating as one in oneness
As the lord of five elements, Siva be.
Be the Prophet. Aum Namah Sivaya

All mystics of the ancients, through all cultures, understood Oneness as our association with nature, the sun and the moon. For the Yogis, the five elements that we embody are like sheaths of energy to be mastered. In mastering the five elements, the Yogis can transcend the limits of the body. When we meditate or pray, we dissolve ourselves into Source through the five elements.

Upon reaching the final element of infinity and space, we attain awareness of ourselves being the vast Spirit of Infinity. Within infinity we realize the energy within, the void and that within the atom as One.

Consciousness is the wisdomwisdomwisdom within the five elements.

Consciousness Sutra 79. Grace of Inner Fire, Tapas

In the core of being is the vibrancy of stillness
spinning each thought
from the womb of infinity
to the ocean of Consciousness
in the inner fire.
The master who lights our inner fire is our guru.
in this fire is all the past digested
and fruits all spiritual journeys of temples, caves,
shrines, yagnas, pujas and the presence of all gurus.
invoke and digest the light of grace.
In summoning all of spiritual grace to the now, grow the
inner fire
to master Consciousness.
In the inner fire of grace, Siva be.
Be the Prophet. Aum Namah Sivaya

The foundation of Consciousness is built with Tapas, the meditative inner fire. After all the spiritual awakening, the pilgrimage within, is through the inner fire, through Tapas. Beings like Ramana Maharishi, Guru Ayya, Balayogi, to name a few of the Sages, went into the Tapas mode for years together, digesting the inner fire light. They emerged as Masters of Consciousness, able to alight Consciousness in an instant to anyone who sought awakening. They also shared the Grace within Consciousness that they inherited through their many years of meditation.
In our daily inner journey of even a few minutes of Tapas, we are able to tap the pre-existing immense Consciousness of masters, alongside with summoning all the blessings received of past spiritual journeys in the now moment of Tapas.

Tapas is an accelerator of Consciousness.

Consciousness Sutra 80. Samadhi

In each breath is the swirl of Consciousness –
the ascending hooded serpent of cosmic knowing.
Inhaling from the roots of the moon breath, swirling into the sun
breath in the exhale above,
through the third eye, be the witness of the blossom of the lotus above.
Each breath unlocks the eternal wisdom's breath beyond breath realm.
Eternal wisdom of all Sages is in the ocean of bliss of each moment in samadhi.
In awareness of being light, Consciousness as lotus blossoms.
In the breathless awake, Siva be.
Be the Prophet. Aum Namah Sivaya

Siddhars like Mahasivaswamy could in a moment step into the state of samadhi and anyone near him would also be pulled into a similar state of ecstasy and stillness.
In his teachings was the unlocking of breath's secret to attain the highest of Consciousness, the samadhi state. When we inhale with the left nostril (moon breath) – from the roots and swirl our breath to exhale from the right side, (sun breath) aware of the blossom of the crown of lights above, through the third eye, we enable a cosmic mind. Attainment of the inner fire to step into samadhi is mighty Grace of several lifetimes as forever, Consciousness like lotus has blossomed inside of us.

In the mind absorbed in cosmic union is Consciousness, the sun of awareness shining.

Consciousness Sutra 81. Mantra: Seeds of Consciousness

The infinite dwells in the seed of a single thought
as the energy within matter and spirit.
Acquiring more intensity as with time
through tapas – the inner mantra fire cooks
the mind to expand Consciousness.
Over years of focus in carrying the infinite as
sacred presence dwelling in one thought magnifies each
thought
to be mighty seeds.
Potent is the blessed reality of a Yogi.
Cooked mantra grace is the many seeds of Consciousness
serve Consciousness seeds in the grace of mantra shared.
In the mantra as presence Siva be.
Be the Prophet. Aum Namah Sivaya

The single thought is activated through the chant of the mantra that holds the infinite. When we chant, we are able to experience the meditative no-thought void mind state with the luxury of joy. When we chant, we alight joy as it awakens our heart-song like a nursery rhyme. With years of chanting, the resonance of the mantras get potent in energies and when shared, it awakens joy in others as a form of a subtle initiation. Chanting mantras is an effective tool of enhanced Consciousness. For all of the Eastern philosophy's history, Consciousness was conveyed by Sages mostly through the mantras.

Blessed to receive the mantra, awaken to Consciousness.

Consciousness Sutra 82. Break Free

In human, entwined with
mind exists pure joy
of the inner fire awake
in the shrine of our being.
Tending this pure joyfulness of Divine union,
we surrender the mind of baggage, including the body,
to awaken to the freedom of our vaster being
of infinite Consciousness, unhindered by trivial mortality.
It is the eternal vibrancy of being spirit that rejuvenates the
shrine of our being.
In being the shrine awake in purpose we serve humanity,
fulfilled and inspired.
In attaining the mind of joy and the form of joy,
Consciousness is humanity's joyful blessings.
In joys of freedom to be Consciousness, Siva be!
Be the Prophet. Aum Namah Sivaya

Poets and philosophers of all cultures and religions mention one word more often than any other word – and that is freedom. To be 'liberated' is a Yogic terminology. It all begins with alighting the state of joy within ourselves as a sacred inner fire wherein we surrender the mind and all the thoughts of realities. Growing this fire of bliss and then becoming the form of bliss by way of body we attain Consciousness. We understand ourselves as the shrine that houses the sacred inner fire of Source that serves all of humanity.

Consciousness is the blossom of joy's wisdom that sets us free to Be.

Consciousness Sutra 83. Passion of Inner Union

The lotus of our realities
is fueled by passion from the inner-most desire.
In the passion of the heart is the crown's blossom.
In the passion of the crown is the knowing of third eye.
In the passion the third eye is the blessings of the heart.
In Consciousness is the heart's dream humanity's reality.
In this passion is all angelic realms' collective intent of
humanity's purpose to be angelic.
humanity's dreams are fulfilled by through Consciousness
with each thought the mighty seed, nurtured by the grace of
the we.
In the grace of the we, the fire of Siva be.
Be the Prophet. Aum Namah Sivaya

There are different layers of realization. The first layer is to wake up to be a Conscious being. From here as in Consciousness, our journey to being whole and free awakens. The most potent of all realization is our life's highest purpose – our heart's calling. When we align ourselves to our heart's work, our crown chakra, the thousand petals of awareness of joy, blossoms. Our third eye brings focus to channel the vast Divine energies into human realities. Our heart opens to be the Consciousness that sustains the passion of the vision and in manifesting this reality.

Passion is the wheel of Consciousness.

Consciousness Sutra 84. Grace of Stillness

Cosmic union creates
the wings to fly above the mind.
The wings to fly evolves to glide in grace of stillness.
The joyful vibrant stillness lofty gift is Consciousness.
Guided by heart's rapture as wisdom of joy that attains stillness,
master Consciousness.
Meditate.
In stillness is effortlessness that consumes all the universes – in being.
In the dance within, stillness of Siva be.
Be the Prophet. Aum Namah Sivaya

Through history, through every region of the world, there has been a similar experience of joy, bliss or euphoria when anyone has connected the mind to the cosmic union. In Divine Grace is the next state of evolution of Consciousness and that is stillness. In stillness is the ability to consume the supreme elation of cosmic union as Consciousness. In awakening to Consciousness, we understand stillness to be intensified meditation. Consciousness is nurtured and grown from meditation.

Even a few moments of stillness of the mind, its thoughts and our expansion into the infinite realm lights the fire of Consciousness.

Consciousness Sutra 85. Be the Mahatma

As the many multiplied to be one,
we are multitude realities of Consciousness.
The awake soul is the immense giant, the mahatma.
the angelic oneness of Consciousness
invokes all Sages of Consciousness as our intent.
Each thought is the gift of ancient presence born of a mind of
Consciousness.
We are the thread of intent of oneness that defines time from
our collective timeless being.
The 'we' replaces the 'i' in our intent, thought and doings.
Each a multitude of many the many mahatmas in
Consciousness.
humanity's gift is in uplifting grandness of each thought.
The mahatma, as Siva be.
Be the Prophet. Aum Namah Sivaya

Siddhar Rajaswamy, Nandhiji's Guru, would teach: 'Your own mind is your Guru. Understand your mind as the medium through which all great Masters of Consciousness can be invoked. Each thought then becomes a Guru. Consciousness of the masters then understands the sacred dharma as in lifting humanity, the intent of all masters of ages.' In understanding Consciousness as the mighty potential of being the presence of all Masters of Consciousness, we align ourselves to the immenseness of who we truly are. In attaining the wisdom of the Spirit, the 'I' 'Me' 'Mine' of ego dissolves away and instead, we represent all of humanity as 'We' and 'Ours'. As we represent the past of all Consciousness in the now, we lead humanity, with the guiding presence of all the masters before us. Our thoughts are mighty in what it is capable of manifesting.

Consciousness is the Guru that guides and paves the way to perfect thoughts, aligned realities of goodness and dissolves ignorance to enhance more of Consciousness.

Consciousness Sutra 86. Realms of Turiya

Our each moment is expanded and yet not enough
to confine the vast being of ours within the twenty-four
hours of time.
In the elegance of the flow, we are the infinite and finite in
the dance
as the super mind of Consciousness.
In the Divine realm of Turiya,
we dissolve the sun and moon of time into timelessness
that contains the universe.
Each moment of Turiya is mighty inspiration, immense joy
and enormous doings. above the mind, liberated, each
moment is reality's masterpiece.
Each masterpiece of doing furthering humanity beyond
confines of the past.
In Turiya as Siva's grace, be.
Be the Prophet. Aum Namah Sivaya

The state of Turiya that Sages call 'the sleepless sleep'- is a super-Consciousness state of the mind. While Sages step into the Turiya state with ease through meditation, every ordinary person too does step into brief moments of Turiya. An artist painting; a baby suckling on her mother; a writer writing; and a child playing are some examples. When we step into the Turiya state we forget hunger, sometimes heat and cold, and forgo sleep. We are in the 'flow' that enables us to accomplish amazing realities in the timelessness when our innate talents awaken and we are in astates of inspiration.

To attain the Turiya state of mind is Mastery of Consciousness.

Consciousness Sutra 87. Empowered Transformation

Karma's hard knocks make us teachers of dharma.
teachers come forth in various disguises – as human, and as circumstances.
the first painful knocks lead us to prayers.
Then as pilgrim we journey to seek more of Source.
Then we awaken to being the spirit, Source essence.
As awake, our karma of past transforms to dharma of the now.
Consciousness is dharma. Consciousness evolves.
Consciousness is the now.
In dharma evolving, as Siva be.
Be the Prophet. Aum Namah Sivaya

The journey to Source and Consciousness begins at first for most people with being beaten by life to seek the Divine for solutions as prayers. Slowly but surely, we begin to seek more of the Divine for Peace of mind. From here we graduate to wanting the cosmic union state of mind for all times. In this journey is the discarding and utilization of the past, its limits and the imprints to attain the evolved now moment – with our Karma transformed to Dharma as Consciousness.

A perfect example for this is the story of Helen Keller.

The name of Helen Adams Keller is known around the world as a symbol of courage in the face of overwhelming odds, yet she was much more than a symbol. She was a woman of luminous intelligence, high ambition and great accomplishment. She devoted her life to helping others. Helen Keller was only 19 months old when she contracted a fever that left her blind and deaf. When she was almost seven years old, her parents engaged Anne Sullivan to be her tutor; Anne was able to evoke and help develop the child's enormous intelligence. Miss Keller won numerous honors, including honorary university degrees, the Lion's Humanitarian Award, the Presidential Medal of Freedom, and election to the

Women's Hall of Fame. During her lifetime, she was consistently ranked near the top of 'most admired' lists.

In awakening, Consciousness transforms karma to Dharma

Consciousness Sutra 88. The Guru

The awake mind, Consciousness, is the guru.
Behind each thought is the proximity to Source
that defines the potency of thought
and the stream of realities unfolded.
Blessed by the auspiciousness of Consciousness
our mind ascends to be the guru, the inner guru.
As bridge between the experience and the experiencer is the
'i'
of Consciousness, the guru.
As wisdom form, Siva be.
Be the Prophet. Aum Namah Sivaya

All Masters of Consciousness, as Prophets, give us teachings to arrive at Consciousness, the direct experience with Source. After reaching the destination of connecting with Source, we awaken to our heart's inner wisdom. Our inner Guru is now awake. This inner Guru is Consciousness. Teachers like Ayya awaken our own inner fire to enable us a journey through Consciousness. In our journey through Consciousness, we become the Guru by awakening our inner Guru as Consciousness.

In the awakening of Consciousness is our own inner lamp awake to be the Guru.

Consciousness Sutra 89. Astral Travel

Pilgrimages to sacred shrines & places enables the digestion of light.
Astral travel as siddhi serves as pilgrimages to visit and revisit places of worship. astral pilgrimages enable the grace of stillness as light is digested.
The astral pilgrimage to holy places is grace of empowerment
to merge with the Source drinking the ever-flowing grace.
As a bee seeking nectar, journey as spirit to all shrines to be the one.
Merge in the sanctum sanctorum of all shrines to be the pillar of light –
of Consciousness.
In the pilgrimage to one, Siva be.
Be the Prophet. Aum Namah Sivaya

We possess many super-natural powers for a good reason. When we utilize such powers to enhance Consciousness, we align ourselves to the Divine logic of such powers, called Siddhis. It is never a good reason to utilize such extra powers for any other purpose other than to seek more of Divinity and do goodness for humanity.

When we do astral travel as a Divine cosmic journey to revisit or visit sacred shrines, we are like a bee. The nectar is in the delving into the 'I am' experience within each shrine. The Grace of such digestion of light is the ability to sit still in the joys of the inner dance of light.

Consciousness is the Grace of being One.

Consciousness Sutra 90. Evolve

When Confucius sang, 'we live here as in an egg – either we evolve or we decay',
the words awaken us to the Siddhar wisdom of human birth.
The precious human birth holds the gift of transcendence and to evolve
to be the angelic liberated being.
Decay of the mind is karmic entrapment as limited by patterns of the past.
Decay is the inability to grasp the finest treasure of birth – to evolve.
The Yogic freedom to grow and incubate higher Consciousness
is the supreme blessings of this human birth.
Awakening mother Kundalini to transform human realities evolve in the magic of Grace.
As the angelic Consciousness, Siva be.
Be the Prophet. Aum Namah Sivaya

For a Siddhar Yogi, time is precious. It is important to utilize every moment to evolve into ever higher states of Consciousness. We understand stagnancy as decay and for growth, we constantly discard the old to welcome change as the new.

We tap into the magical abilities to evolve. 'Every saint was a sinner in the past' – this maxim holds true. In the intensity of our Yogic pursuit we evolve quickly. By evolving, we know that is the greatest gift of a lifetime we could ever receive – to be angelic as a being of Consciousness.

Consciousness is ever evolving and dynamic in transforming.

Consciousness Sutra 91. Breath of the Now

Liberating ourselves each day into the euphoria of
Consciousness adorn the infinite sky of the mind.
With each breath in the awareness of inhale from the roots,
straighten the spine from the tailbone upwards.
With the spine alight and the body as a pyramid,
be the center of Harmony, tranquility and core wisdom.
Each breath straightening the spine, liberate to be spirit.
Every waking hour, be aware of breath in its journey
to the vastness of the mind that is expanding Consciousness.
As liberated, Siva be
Be the Prophet. Aum Namah Sivaya

Each breath has within it a journey that begins from the roots, climbs up through the spine alighting the pathway to reach above to the mind that is expanding in Consciousness. When we breathe with awareness, our spine straightens and our body is in the Yogic relaxation. A straight spine causes the foundation of a mind of Consciousness. In activating a mind that identifies itself with the infinity of the sky is to attain clarity of a meditative mind.

In every breath with awareness of the inhale, retention and exhale, we grow the cosmic mind of Consciousness.

Consciousness Sutra 92. Child of the Cosmos

In the perceived forms of infinity is the guru, Consciousness.
When inspired, align to be the guru in the knowing
when awake, we are the six dimensional being.
Uniting the three-dimensional Source
and the three-dimensional physical,
as the cosmic male and Divine female entwined,
the five senses multiply to be six, the extra Divine sense of unique genius.
Awake, be the son/daughter of god/Source, the guru – as Consciousness.
Summon the power of the infinite one
to be the grand dynamic realities of the six-dimensional invoked and be.
As father and mother of the offspring, Consciousness, Siva be.
Be the Prophet. Aum Namah Sivaya

Through Yogic breathing, we kindle Mother Kundalini. The left breath of the moon and the sun breath of the right are rivers that lead to the ocean of light. By way of arousing the inner fire, we are awakening to be the daughter/son of the Source. Lord Muruga is symbolized as the dynamic energies, enterprise, instant evolution and victory of endeavor. When we awaken, we are the six dimensional being endowed with the gift of extrasensory perception (ESP), the sixth sense, the Siddhis. The Siddhis awakened is unique for each of us as the innate talent of genius switched on.

In attainment of Consciousness, we awaken to the immense being we are capable of amazing truth.

Consciousness Sutra 93. Expand Mind's Potency

Beneath the Yogic mind rests the foundation of grace
built through tapas, dharma and karma
which determine each thought;
the realities destined and created;
and the power to be in the now.
The fire of tapas is intensified bliss
which dissolves karma through dharma.
In joys of the inner fire that expands potency of the mind adorned,
create the empowering now as blessings of humanity.
Expanding grace of being, Siva be.
Be the Prophet, Aum Namah Sivaya

Consciousness from the Yogic perspective has a simple formula of uniting Tapas with the awareness of karma and observance of dharma to arouse the Grace of Consciousness. When we are in the joys of Tapas, Mother Kundalini as the Source of Consciousness awakens. When we are mindful of the laws of Karma, our Consciousness is allowed to grow. When we realize Dharma as in our thought and action we expand Consciousness exponentially. The more of Consciousness, the more we unite these three powerful dimensions into inspired play of each moment. Consciousness forever grows.

To multiply Consciousness at all times is Consciousness.

Consciousness Sutra 94. Siddhis of Consciousness

With the highest purpose actualized, Consciousness is well planted.
Consciousness is blessings of an empowered mind
that spins realities tuned by the primal vibrations held.
Siddhis awaken with Consciousness blossoming.
in Dharma, Siddhis nurture Consciousness
in Karma, Siddhis hamper the roots of Consciousness.
As wise, step beyond Dharma and Karma to attune to pure Consciousness.
Dissolving every layer of attachments, the realm of Consciousness
gifts each moment the miracle of now, the ultimate siddhi of Grace.
Dissolved, be Siva, as Grace.
Be the Prophet. Aum Namah Sivaya

In our daily inner journey to Consciousness, we witness miracles. Extra sensory perception (ESP) awakens. Texts make mention of eight major Siddhis classified as: Anima (the ability to shrink in size); Mahima (illimitability of size); Lagima (lightness and ability to levitate); Garima (to increase in weight); Prapthi (ability to fulfill any desires); Prakasyam (power of irresistible will); Isithavam (supremacy over laws of nature); and Vasithavam (dominion over the five elements).These eight Siddhis are called the Ashtama Siddhis. However, the teachings of the Siddhars discourage use of any of the Siddhis, including smaller Siddhis such as fortune telling. Any time a Siddhi is utilized, there is Karma accrual that cannot be avoided. Our way of worship is in dissolving our mind into the Divine.

When we dissolve our mind and any Siddhi with it, leaving it all to the purity of Divine will, our Consciousness is elevated further and every thought becomes a miracle and scripture.

Consciousness Sutra 95. Oneness of humanity as Consciousness

As the swan glides effortlessly over himalayan limitations
so flows our ever expanding Consciousness to resolve
limits of our own mind and realities and as that of
humanity's.
The wings are the sacred diaphragm of intent of each of us
awake to become humanity in Consciousness.
The vastness of oneness empowers the wings.
We are ever expanding Consciousness potent
in alighting to be one humanity.
The wholeness of humanity, as Siva be.
Be the Prophet. Aum Namah Sivaya

In our journey is empowerment of Consciousness with understanding of the flow of Grace. When we seek Grace for ourselves, Grace flows in trickles. When we seek Grace for a vaster representation of oneness, as humanity, Grace flows as a flooded river. In our prayer, contemplation and meditation, the intent held for all of humanity is aligned with the invoking of all Masters of Consciousness of the past and present summoned. Collective Consciousness amplifies itself to lift all. In this age of Consciousness, we are the arrow heads of the dynamic alighting Consciousness that serves humanity selflessly as Divine instruments.

In the rain of Grace invoked for all, our own tree of Consciousness grows.

Consciousness Sutra 96. Inspiration of Oneness

Knowing limitlessness is Consciousness
and its mastery is in the inspiration to expand even further.
Human Karma burns naturally and effortlessly
as darkness absorbed by the light of Consciousness.
Hold hands as one to bring humanity to our primal fires
of Consciousness that liberates us as Peace in realization.
Our boundless oneness conquers the past
to usher the new for mother earth.
The angelic benediction is the fire of inspiration
of the oneness of Consciousness in our being one.
Be the Prophet. Aum Namah Sivaya

All Sages of the past history of humanity have had a singular intent as Consciousness for all of humanity. Whenever a higher-conscious realized master appeared in each society across the globe, irrespective of which culture or religion it was, humanity has progressed. However, there was a lot of resistance in the past to the advent of higher Consciousness, is evident in the crucifixion, killing and assassination of these masters throughout the thread of history. This resistance to Consciousness is now slowly giving way. We are now able to understand the Consciousness of these masters as our very own. The blessing of Consciousness liberates humanity from ignorance. The wisdom of oneness of Consciousness is real Peace that uplifts all on Planet Earth.

By being one in intent for all on planet Earth, we are blessed by the inspiration of the Divine Oneness to be One, as Consciousness.

Consciousness Sutra 97. Each Breath

In the ladder of wisdom is breath and its gates.
These are gates that open ever wider gates – into samadhi and beyond.
Which awakens us to the million minds alight
as each mighty thought of knowing. lead breath to Consciousness.
Set intent within the empty space between the exhale and the inhale.
Set the intent to surrender and receive and
inhale from the roots below.
Course exhale upwards as in intent to be the limitless Consciousness.
exhaling through the spine alight,
open the third eye gate by being the dweller, dancing.
Seated in vibrant stillness of knowing.
Be the dance in the breathless breath of stillness in the third eye.
In the focus of the million minds, Siva be.
Be the Prophet. Aum Namah Sivaya

What the Yogis who do Tapas continuously do, can be done by each of us with every breath. By constant awareness within each breath, by way of inhaling from the roots and exhaling through the spine with focus on the third eye, we are kindling Consciousness, the highest state of the mind, which is Guru. The Guru here is the wisdom from within that is awoken. By being aware of each breath, we utilize our lungs to oxygenate ourselves. In the process of breathing deeply we expand the mind's potential to think better. When we utilize the heightened awareness to expand Consciousness continuously, we are like Sages who are able to be in perpetual meditation even while involving in activities like driving, writing or speaking, 24/7.

Consciousness is in the awake state of mind, obtained in each breath.

Consciousness Sutra 98. Ride Consciousness

Each day's roller coaster of the mind
has the highs and lows and its rider.
From this roller coaster springs thoughts of the rider that expands Consciousness.
As a Yogi, we are the rider enjoying roller coaster through each
breath to ride the highs in inspiration
and in the natural mind cycle unfolds,
we ride the lows plunging into depth of surrender
and attain mind's wholeness in the plunge.
To attain that alchemy of surrender to wholeness is potent Consciousness.
The rider's vehicle of mind then glides as Consciousness
as the engine creating realities so desired.
As the bull of Siva, ride and be.
Be the Prophet. Aum Namah Sivaya

The mind flips the breath five times each day to the right nostril, the sun breath (according to the teachings of Siddhar Bhoganathar). This is a natural process for all humans. The breath flipping to the right, to the sun breath, allows for enhanced focus, meditation and ability to connect with our higher self. When the breath flips to the left, the moon breath, we are tired and it's time to rejuvenate. With the breath changing sides is the mind that goes up and down. As a Yogi, ride the mind through the rivers of breath. When it is the sun breath of optimism, utilize this breath for its inspiration and focus. When it is the moon breath of depression or dullness, surrender the mind to the Source by ways of prayer, puja or silence in uniting to the Source.

Understanding the mind's cycle as meant to be utilized in life, as a Yogi, guide the mind through breath to Consciousness and be.

Consciousness Sutra 99. wisdom of Tantiram

In awakening the roots of innermost passion,
the magic of genius and immense manifestations arises.
The Divine imprint in each as the human purpose awakens the knowing
that kindles passion to evolve us to be the angel
in uniting the Source with human reality, is tantiram, the sacred union to evolve.
In tantiram is the cosmic grace and our roots passion igniting oneness –
one as wisdom, one as intellect, one as in doings.
As in mastery of time through the knowing of timelessness,
define the joys of realities as in sacredness of passion.
In grace of tantiram, Siva be.
Be the Prophet. Aum Namah Sivaya

Great leaders of history and in today's world shape humanity in realities due to the enormously awakened root chakra. In realizing our heart's purpose, our roots awaken the intense energies of passion to make our dreams come true. In the roots, alive as the fire of passion, and the Spirit as the wisdom, is Tantiram – that alights joy. The inner fire of Tapas too likewise kindles the states of joy. This joy that comes from the union of the cosmic infinity with our innermost finite of being is Tantiram.
The wisdom of Tantiram is known as the primal energy within ourselves that when aroused, rises upwards and blossoms all that is within and around us as it ascends. Below, at the base chakra, is the primal energy that can make a baby; above is the Divine energy that manifests thoughts.

As with being the joys of passionate fires of Tantiram magnify Consciousness.

Consciousness Sutra 100. Tree of Consciousness

With each passing day of the Divine seeking
the inner journey sprouts newer leaves
which reach out to the sun as the crown chakra,
and the tender plant of Consciousness grows to be the
mighty tree.
Tree of Consciousness is manifested through fires of the
inner journey, tapas,
offering shade for all of humanity.
As natural as to evolve from plant to tree is for human to
become angelic.
As in being, serving humanity, Siva be.
Be the Prophet. Aum Namah Sivaya

As we ascend, as in the spirit awakening experience, our crown chakra as petals blossom much like a tree's leaves connecting to sunlight. We grow from the fragile seeking to the robust knowing; like a plant to a tree, we also grow in the Consciousness to understand our innate purpose – to serve humanity – much like the shade of the tree to serve anyone who seeks it.

The innate nature of Consciousness is Dharma and being at the receiving end of Grace.

Consciousness Sutra 101. Giant of Breath.

Igniting the roots through the inhale.
The retention of breath, ascend.
At the navel is the guru above body Consciousness.
At the heart is unconditional love to receive, give and be.
At the throat is the clearance of all karmic imprints of limitations.
At the crown is the infinity of ecstasy in being.
With awareness converged at the third eye exhale.
The breath of the immense being is truth of who we are – that yields to the breath-beyond-breath vastness of Consciousness
As eternal of breath, Siva be
Be the Prophet. Aum Namah Sivaya

In breath is the thought stream regulated. Our ability to be happy, optimistic, inspired and in tune with who we really are, is in each breath's journey. In every aware breath, when we inhale from the roots and in the retention attentively, we are waking up the inner fire of Mother Kundalini. As the breath like a serpent climbs upwards, each energy center, the chakra points blossom transforming our inner and outer world. The navel chakra is seldom known outside the mystical Yogic knowledge. Awakening the navel chakra, we go beyond body and mind Consciousness to attain stillness. Likewise, the heart chakra awakens us to being love, that like the key to the door of the cosmos unlocks the throat chakra. In the throat chakra, we break free of karmic patterns of past lives that unveils the vastness of our being in the sparkle of the crown. In the third eye, we unite the infinite with the finite of our focus.

Each breath, we are formed of, is magnificent Consciousness; the giant.

Consciousness Sutra 102. Bridge to Be.

Each day's journey begins in seeking in humility of a
sanyasin as the awareness of temporary
with the need for the eternal nature of all things.
The need to Source connect.
Awakening from the sleeping mind as Source connected, the sanyasin becomes the emperor.
Aligning duality of the human seekings and the cosmic union
is the bridge of Consciousness.
In mastery of Consciousness is Harmony of union in seeking and being.
Between seeking and the being is the awakening from time and karma
to be timelessness in dharma.
Shortness of life as in the flash of an eyelid – is time.
In timelessness, each moment is in the infinity being.
The bridge between strengthens with frequency of this journey daily with
grace of humility and surrender paving to be the fountain of wisdom.
Be the emperor having conquered time, being the bridge that is reality.
The causal of reality, as Siva be.
Be the Prophet. Aum Namah Sivaya

Each morning, when we wake up from sleeping, the mind needs raising up through the layers as a natural start-up process. In the first instance is the Grace of humility and surrender to seek more of the Divine/Infinity/Consciousness. Utilizing Yogic tools, we climb into the state of Being. The bridge between seeking and being is like a muscle that gets stronger with daily practice. To go back and forth across this 'bridge' is important, as lack of humility and surrender can make our wisdom stagnant, and stagnant wisdom becomes ignorance quickly. Upon realizing our Source connect, we awaken to the Grace of timelessness and our immense being of purpose and then, in human realities we do not waste a single moment.

Consciousness is the Grace of understanding the Oneness of it all, as in Being.

Consciousness Sutra 103. I Am

We nurture and incubate this mind into the fertile thresholds of Turiya,
the sacred realm immersed with Source/infinity.
Here our mind expands enough to hold the vastness of ourselves as truth of our being,
the immense being, pure Consciousness.
– understand ourselves as in the vastness of trillions of light years and more,
having taken birth and in this moment for a good reason.
– climb within infinity where our inner music dancing flows in a mind as clear as the sky.
– merge into infinity's vibrant inner music beginning with breath's loud song.
– express gratitude on cellular level for the body and gratitude for our reality. emerging as gratitude expressed of each thought.
With the body as clothes and the mind as the vehicle,
feel the immenseness of our being as in saying 'i am' the spirit.
As spirit acknowledged we are the grandness of soul, the mahatma.
As spirit, Siva be.
Be the Prophet. Aum Namah Sivaya

The 'I Am' experience of all Prophets and Masters of Consciousness before us is potent in realizing a mind that can utilize Consciousness to enhance more of Consciousness. In the state of Turiya is the dissolving of the mind into infinity. A mind of crystal clarity has no thought or a singular thought of intense focus. Attaining a Turiya state of mind is through little steps such as

- In preparing the mental vibrations with understanding ourselves greater than any circumstance around us;
- Expanding ourselves to the vastness of infinity where our own breath becomes the external 'music' that

reveals to us our inner music within the 'silence' of infinity.

- Enter within states of gratitude through our body Consciousness and our awareness of life, our mind is at ease to align to infinity.
- Understand ourselves as the Spirit wearing a body and utilizing the mind. Consciousness is God/Source/Infinity as in the wisdom of Being.

Consciousness Sutra 104. Grace of Stillness, Sthira

Each moment and each Yogic posture contains the center of grace, the sthira.
In sthira is vibrant stillness of Harmony, the supreme state of zero.
As is each form of ours held as a pyramid of stability upright that holds the sthira within,
as the center of gravity.
Sit and walk knowing our body form as the pyramid aware of the center,
the sthira within that tends the inner fire.
Through each Yogic posture, attain sthira
to drink the nectar of each posture's gift.
As in the center of centers, Siva be.
Be the Prophet. Aum Namah Sivaya

Each moment, when we stand, sit or walk, we are attentive to the energy field we are in. When we consider our form as a pyramid and our form is perfectly poised, stable, upright and in balance – this is the first step. Next is the attention we bring to the center within that posture and the attainment of ease, Harmony and calm of breath. This is in Sanskrit is called 'sthira'. Every posture of Yoga has a power within it as a gift to be received. When doing the Yogic asanas, likewise, when we seek the sthira within each posture, we attain the gift each posture contains.

As in observing sthira at all times, Consciousness is tended as the inner fire grown from the bed of Harmony.

Consciousness Sutra 105. Each Thought the Master

Each master of Consciousness before us was like a rain-bearing cloud
with intent to rain Consciousness to all around them.
Most masters were crucified, assassinated or killed.
Christ, Abraham Lincoln, Mahatma Gandhi and Martin Luther King are the few of the
countless fearless masters named.
When life is terminated unnaturally; the spirit of the deceased lingers on.
Masters of Consciousness live aware of being the spirit with eternal intent and
when their life is cut short, their powerful intent lives on.
Invoke to be all masters of higher Consciousness tuned to the magnified intent of goodness
for humanity and each thought arising is the guru, the master.
As the guru, Siva be
Be the Prophet. Aum Namah Sivaya

Siddhar Rajaswamy's every-day prayer for humanity is through the Siddhar yagna twice a day invoking all Masters of Consciousness into human reality. He would explain thus: 'When you invoke these masters into the human realities, they make themselves present as powerful thoughts and realities. Imagine one Christ who created Christianity as a religion. Imagine invoking all these masters. Our intent is not more of Hindus, Christians or Muslims but instead, more of Christs, Mohammads and Krishnas for each of us to be. Each of our thoughts become the Guru.'

Print images of beings whom we want to emulate and have these images placed where we work. When we invoke Masters of CConsciousness by honoring their presence by having images or mentally invoking them, we can be sure that they will be present as the singular Consciousness we possess.

As sum total of all masters of Consciousness in intent, be the unified Consciousness of One.

Consciousness Sutra 106. Highest Teachings of Masters

Life teachings of all Prophets reveal crispness of wisdom of the moment,
the people and Consciousness of the times.
No Prophet followed another.
Rules of collective intellectual ego are often broken as Consciousness evolves.
Followers of Prophets understood the words of wisdom as their own unspoken truths from the heart
so then inspired to follow the teachings as their own.
Awakening to the prevailing Consciousness of now, listening to truth within,
as Prophet - write your own scripture and follow it exclusively by yourself.
As Prophet, Siva be.
Be the Prophet. Aum Namah Sivaya

Beings like Christ, Mahatma Gandhi and almost all Masters of Consciousness is easily invoked by prayers, contemplation and meditation as their vibrant presence is more than willing to serve. Siddhar Rajaswamy would often tell a story of his past with his Guru, Siddhar Kakaneswar. He and his Guru would spend days together in the forest. Every evening when his Guru would meditate, all animals including, deer, rabbits, wild boars birds would gather around them with a vibrancy of Peace and Tranquility.

Siddhar Rajaswamy once asked his Guru, 'I see all these living beings come to you in Peace. But there seems to be something more that that my eyes can see. What is it?' Siddhar Kakaneswar then said, 'Yes, all beings seek Peace. So when they sense Peace as Consciousness it is natural for them to gravitate towards Peace. But also, the angels and all higher beings too come and circle around. For them, it is an opportunity to evolve. They are stuck in a stagnant realm with progress possible only by taking human birth. When these higher beings recognize a conscious human, they wish to serve this being as it is their natural desire to evolve.'

Understand this truth as we realize how precious human life is as in its potential to evolve and how all higher conscious angelic beings are so willing to serve.'

Consciousness Sutra 107. Eat Love

All masters of Consciousness resonate at a vibrancy
of love, Peace, tranquility, Harmony and all aspects of goodness.
Consciousness of past validating eating meat is today's ignorance
as Consciousness has grown exponentially in humanity's evolution in wisdom. Consciousness is energy.
Food is energy input, each thought is energy output and
the bed of mind as memory and thinking pattern is energy is retained.
Eat love and compassion to be the wisdom of love, Peace and oneness.
The energy of Consciousness is fed by our eating habits.
As in sensitivity of oneness to be one, Siva be
Be the Prophet. Aum Namah Sivaya

What we eat is what we are. With science now advocating vegetarianism, we can look towards food of compassion (devoid of killing, pain and injury to another living being) with an even more rational mind beyond emotions. Food is a vibrant energy that is the medicine for the body and mind. Sages of the East have for thousands of years advised vegetarian food to enhance Consciousness. From improving memory and intellect, to curbing anger and negative emotions attributed to vegetarianism, the masters of the East attribute deeper meditation to a diet that does not contain imprints of fear of a dying animal. The list of conscious beings who were vegetarians through history is long. However, we can be certain that a more intelligent diet as vegetarian is awakening as awareness especially among the younger generation as the right choice.

Consciousness always multiplies Consciousness and through the wisdomwisdomwisdom of eating conscious food, planet earth will see goodness flourish.

Consciousness Sutra 108. We are Consciousness

We are the truth within all religions.
We are the collective Consciousness of all masters.
We are the ones we have been waiting for.
We worship the lamp within ourselves.
We honor all paths to Consciousness.
We are Peaceful. we are non-violent.
We uphold the equality of all humanity.
We utilize intelligent means to protect ourselves against ignorance.
We cherish the sacredness of the equality of the feminine and masculine
we are the scientists of every profession and the priests to our own Consciousness.
We are the messengers of Peace heralding the millions more born each day.
We honor the Divine in every name and the namelessness.
We pray for humanity, planet earth and all the living.
We are kind, sensitive, charitable and innately good.
We meditate and draw our wisdom from within.
We are compassionate to all the living.
We arc the timelessness defining time.
We sustain and nourish mother earth.
We are the dynamics of change.
We know our heart's purpose.
We are Consciousness.
We are the liberated.
We lead humanity.
We are one

Consciousness was victorious by celebrating all paths to Consciousness and being One humanity.

PROLOGUE: VICTORY & DECLARATION OF CONSCIOUSNESS FOR HUMANITY

For Nandhiji, the most inspiring work ahead in these shared moments has been the role of enhancing Consciousness.

In 2008 Nandhiji led the Opening Inaugural Sacred Fire of Bhakti Fest, the 'Spiritual Woodstock' of the West was launched by visionary, Sridhar Silberfein. The date of the opening was 11 September and it was an occasion to commemorate the disaster of humanity's ignorance – a terrorist attack in the name of God.

It was a powerful moment in time as Nandhiji led all the participants to sing and invoke the name of Allah as a sacred name of Consciousness. This invocation was unique and perhaps one of the most consciously powerful invocations in present day. It was designed to create an understanding of God/Source/Allah as Consciousness and love. It was also designed to bring awareness to the ignorance of human minds stuck in belief systems that are programmed to repeat this tragedy in the name of God and religion.

The name of Allah was invoked with the intent that all present would come together as one, as collective humanity in prayer. The first intent of the prayer was for each participant to declare themselves and all of humanity to be the Prophet and messenger of Peace. The second intent was that by invoking God/Allah as Consciousness, the ignorance of those who interpret the scriptures from its medieval beliefs to be collaborated with violence and jihad, will be conquered. This way, the essence of Consciousness within each religion is awakened to its true nature. Every participant in the sacred circle of Bhakti Fest brought this heart's prayer to a single focus. Many wept. It was perhaps the only public ceremony in the West that took the path of love and Consciousness to address this barbaric illness of humanity, this terrorism. The momentum of Consciousness for planet Earth was set forth from the opening ceremony of Bhakti Fest.

Each year thereafter, Nandhiji would close Bhakti Fest – and its sister event, Shakti Fest – with the intent to amplify Consciousness for all of planet Earth through the potent minds of those celebrating Source union. Year after year and through each gathering, the potency of Consciousness grew as Nandhiji took everyone in the sacred circle to the experience of 'I Am' with an intent for Peace for all of humanity.

It was at Bhakti Fest September 2012 that Nandhiji received the sacred words around his intent of global Peace –*The Declaration of Consciousness Movement* – for all of humanity. At that point in time, it felt as though all Sages of higher Consciousness of the past and present had now the intent of humanity's ultimate aspiration – freedom to Be.

On 21 December, 2012, London hosted the premier of the ground-breaking metaphysical documentary from Starseed Film, '3 MAGIC WORDS,' at the Odeon West End Cinema in Leicester Square. This was followed by a panel discussion with the writer/producer/director of the movie, Michael Perlin, co-producer Maura Hoffman, Theresa Ibis, founder of Indigo Bridge In Service (IBIS), Dolores Cannon and Nandhiji.

'3 Magic Words' evolved from Perlin's personal and lengthy study of metaphysics as he became determined to find a common theme throughout all of ancient mystical teachings. The occasion included a 'blue carpet' with celebrity appearances and a live performance by Lucinda Drayton ('A Hundred Thousand Angels'). http://3magicwordsmovie.com/

This was followed by a Global Meditation led by Sonya Sophia (Sophia School Of Living Arts), a World Peace Prayer conducted by Gudni Gudnason (Modern Mystery School), the announcement of the Declaration of Consciousness by Nandhiji, the reading of this Declaration of Consciousness by 10 year old Simran Serene Chevaliar and the signing of 'The Declaration of Consciousness.'

In London, December 21, 2012, the Declaration of Consciousness was announced!

This was with the purpose to usher humanity to the dawn. On this day, Consciousness won a long, long war, after many battles through the ages of humanity. December 21, 2012, will be recorded in history as the day when the critical mass of Consciousness of humanity was reached – and hence, the Declaration.

This was a proud day for humanity. This realization awakens us to be conscious and declare for ourselves our individual basic freedom.

History shows us that many leaps forward have been made through the ages: Consciousness became more visible in England in 1689, through the Bill of Rights; it evolved in the USA with the Declaration of Independence; and has now returned, in maturity, not just for some, but for the entire planet as the Declaration of Consciousness.

This Declaration of Consciousness relates to the absolute rights of every individual on planet Earth. It specifies an adherence to the Ahimsa principle of non-violence and non-killing; it outlines tolerance of every path to the Divine; it honors the Feminine; it protects and nurtures our children; and it upholds planet Earth as basic Consciousness. (For specifics http://declarationofConsciousness.org)

Historical Thread of Consciousness-
At the time of the birth of Buddha, the court astrologers (astrological birth charts are created even today in most parts of India) looked into the baby boy's horoscope. They saw in his birth chart the immense being he was, and so he was named Siddhartha, the one who is a Siddha. Siddha in Sanskrit and ancient Tamil means a conscious being, one who has mastered the mind.
This Consciousness has never belonged exclusively to any one culture or race. Consciousness is the attainment of connection to the numinous, described by some as Source/God and by some as infinite. All masters who have attained higher Consciousness had a singular wish: to bring Consciousness to all of humanity.

The USA was built on the tenets enshrined in the Declaration of Independence in 1776. Written by Thomas Jefferson and signed by many leaders of that time, the Declaration of Independence is articulate, poetic and enlightened in its core principle that all humans are equal and everyone has the inherent right to be free. Yet, the reality beneath Thomas Jefferson, author and visionary behind this most celebrated of historic documents, is bound by contradiction. Thomas Jefferson was the second largest slave owner in his state, and during his entire lifetime, he freed only two of his hundreds of slaves. So how can the 'Consciousness' within the vision of Declaration of Independence be reconciled?

We need to look deeper into history to find the answer.

The teachings of Jesus Christ came from immense Consciousness that was way beyond his times. That is why he was crucified by a society that could not handle that much truth. If Jesus were with us today each of us would be able to appreciate him, as we are now so much more aligned to the higher wisdom he spoke about; it resonates with our own inner knowing. However, the Jesus of today would speak differently, because Consciousness grows and is ever growing.

When Thomas Jefferson inherited slaves as property from his father, slavery was taken for granted. The first English settlers of 1660 came to America, with slaves. It was socially acceptable to own slaves; not only were they the wheel of economy, but this was the prevailing Consciousness of the times.

Historians have noted that Thomas Jefferson made an effort to be a good master to his slaves, calling them his 'family'. At the time Jefferson wrote the Declaration of Independence, until years after America gained its independence, the ingrained assumption of freedom applied exclusively to the white population. Had Jefferson (who was US President from 1801-1809) taken any step towards emancipation of his slaves, or publicly decried the institution of slavery, his political career would have been wiped out. Jefferson would have risked being assassinated almost immediately.

This truth is evident when in 1865 Abraham Lincoln, aged 56, was assassinated due to the cornerstone policy of his Presidency, the emancipation of slaves, and the end of slavery.

It took another hundred years or more for America to then move towards a higher layer of Consciousness; this happened through the Black Civil Rights movement, headed by Martin Luther King. This movement gained more equality for the entire population of America. He too was assassinated.

The life message of Mahatma Gandhi was that of 'Ahimsa' – the realization of the Oneness of all humans and all living beings. India won its freedom without bloodshed and yet, after attaining the freedom for the nation, Gandhi was assassinated.

However, Consciousness triumphed because of the intent of these higher conscious masters and leaders, to take humanity to the next levels of civilization.

Through history, the seeds of Consciousness planted by the Saints and Sages has grown and is growing further to become the realities we are experiencing today–but not in all countries It is unfortunate that communist countries and dictators have subdued entire populations through fear and force. However, Consciousness and the urge for individual freedom cannot be kept locked up indefinitely; we have seen the collapse of the Berlin Wall and the fall of the Communist regimes of Eastern Europe – and more will inevitably fall

The time has come to state the innermost aspiration of every human on planet Earth. This aspiration is the basic urge and need of every human to want to be free, to want Peace, to create a society of Harmony and conscience and to uphold and sustain Mother Earth. By the Declaration of Consciousness, we frame this common aspiration that is within the heart of all humans. This freedom in the external aspect is one that is not subdued by past beliefs and rules of conduct. The Declaration of Consciousness as an inner directive is that humanity is now ready to evolve to be the Angelic Being – free of the mind and its prejudice, free to understand that we are one with Source/God/Infinity and free to follow our heart's aspiration that embodies basic goodness as one human to another.

The Declaration of Consciousness is an innermost truth; a realization that all humans can evolve to be the higher Consciousness that the Sages of the past and present speak about. Adoption of these truths will mean the attainment of Peace, abundance, non-violence and a just society for all.

This is the new age of Consciousness. We are the Peace Messengers ushering each of us to be the Prophet.

About The Declaration of Consciousness Movement:
The Declaration of Consciousness Movement is a non-profit organization. Contained within its mission is a powerful intent to convey a mesSage of unity Consciousness to all humanity. Its goal is to deliver the Declaration to all national leaders through the United Nations. At the same time, we will actively awaken the grass roots of humanity through music, movies and media.

Should you feel so moved, we deeply value your joining with us in volunteering your time and precious energy in sharing the Declaration of Consciousness as the birth right of every human.

http://declarationofConsciousness.org

GLOSSARY

Ahimsa - The life message of Mahatma Gandhi was Ahimsa. Without any exception, all masters of higher Consciousness recognize Ahimsa as the basic quality of Consciousness. Ahimsa means non-harming, non-killing, non-hurting any other human or living form.

Ananda - The first wave of bliss and joy in realizing the Divine as ourselves, as Spirit having a human experience exposes us to understand the Source of happiness, not from any external circumstance but rather from within. This feeling of ananda is sacred, as this undiluted bliss is the form of Source/God/Lord Siva. Accomplished Yogis acquire the state of ananda and delve even deeper into this bliss state, a state that is one with the highest wisdom, the attribute of Source in human form.

Ancient intent - If we go into the singular intent of all masters of higher Consciousness of past and present, there remains one common intent – that of attainment of higher Consciousness for everybody. Thus, is the ancient intention of higher Consciousness for all that is, is the reason behind all teachings and scriptures of every religion.

Angelic beings - In our human experience, we carry with us the heaven and hell states. In the heaven state, we experience Angelic joys and we are Angelic beings. In the Yogic wisdom of life, we are lucky to be born human so we can evolve into Angelic beings, creating a heaven while we are in physical form. However, climbing above into the spiritual world, we know God/Source to be surrounded by infinite Angelic beings, and each Angelic being can be invoked to be our own higher thoughts and wisdom – hence the importance of invoking higher conscious beings in our prayers to serve us as our own thoughts.

Ascendance – Each inner journey (or even thought process) is akin to climbing up ladders of Consciousness. Any Divine seeking or an exploration of ourself into infinity and stillness is to ascend in Consciousness.

Bhakti - Of all the paths to the Divine, the single most potent of all paths is devotional love, bhakti. Bhakti lights the inner fire and in time, leads us to higher Consciousness with certainty of enlightenment along the way. For the Yogis, bhakti is the most precious gift we can attain, for with bhakti we attain wisdom, and in this wisdom we experience more of bhakti. Devotional love is the essence of the inner journey.

Boon - When we pray for anything and receive an answer to the prayers, it is a boon, a blessing as answer to a prayer or heart's most need.

Cave - Within our own meditation, in the physical and in the mental space, is a cave-like place where we are not bothered anymore by external circumstances or happenings. Yogis initially go to forests and isolated caves to acquire a mind that can find the inner cave. After attaining this inner cave, it does not matter where a Yogi is or what is happening around because in a moment, the mind can be transported to the isolated cave within.

Chakra - Chakras are the energy centers that also hold for us the inner and outer world realities. Each chakra has a defined energy and reality. From the Tamil Siddhar Yogic experiences, the chakras differ from the traditional book information. The first chakra is the root chakra, the Muladhara. The second is the Guru chakra, and the Swadhisthana chakra does not exist. The next chakra is the Manipura chakra of the navel, the Anahata chakra of the heart, Vissudhi chakra of the throat; the Sahasrara of the crown and finally the Ajna chakra of the third eye.

Cosmic beggar - As the Yogi goes deeper into surrender to reach a place where his or her entire survival (as in food and shelter) has been placed before Source, the Yogi becomes a cosmic beggar – begging from Source for every need and living as a bird, provided for by the laws of nature.

Desireless desire - When there is no more desire from the senses and the primary needs, we are led by an inner desire that is guided by Source/God that is in dharma, i.e., a desire to feed the hungry; a desire to simply be alone; and so on.

Dharma - Dharma is to uphold righteousness, right action and right thoughts. When we perform dharma, we are dissolving away our limitations that are in the form of karma, the imprints of past births that imprison us. When awake, from the higher conscious mind we are aware of doing good things and following our purpose and we do dharma that gains us merits and even higher realities for the present and future.

Fullness - In human reality, there is always a search for something or a need for something else. In the Yogic journey, we evolve through fullness as gratitude/contentment /fulfillment for all that we already have. In understanding and appreciating fullness of each moment, we are blessed with inspiration to expand the 'Now' moment further.

Formlessness - The Spirit and the infinite is a mass of energy that a Yogi is in tune with as his/her true Self.

Ganesh - The elephant-headed Divine attribute in the form named as Ganesh, Ganapathy, Vignesh and another thousand names, is the Lord of the root chakra. The root chakra is centered between the anus and the genitals where the inner fire can be lit and grown. The attributes of the root chakra are the five senses, primary needs and the primal urge. The elephant is the five senses and the primal urge. Ganesh represents the elephant head, cut and placed on a human body, to signify transformation as it is in the human birth where we can evolve to be Angelic beings, driven by the inner-most fires.

Genius - The absolute blessing of waking up is to understand ourselves no longer in the confines of our own, limited past, our mind and circumstances, but as freedom to be the vast Spirit and the joys of awareness that flow as wisdom. Each of us upon waking up has a special Divine gift awaiting us in the form a unique Siddhi – a special extraordinary ability that only we can do when bringing our mind to focus on anything that gives us joy. In this process of doing things, we awaken and flow with genius. This genius is the Siddhi, the sixth sense that comes from having conquered the five senses – as the inner most knowing and as the infinite grace of guidance of Source.

Grace - There is the push and pull of energies that transform and evolve us. The push factor is our own individual endeavor and effort. The pull factor is the Divine grace. Without grace, not much progress can be made on the path to Light. Grace is a powerful factor in a Siddhar Yogi's pathway to the Divine as it can be gained through dharmic activities, such as feeding the hungry and doing good deeds. From the state of wisdom, a Yogi knows how to always be at the receiving end of grace with good thoughts, action and humility.

Guru - A Guru is someone, something, or even a thought that awakens us to our higher self. A Guru in the traditional sense is the manifestation of Source/God in human form who destroys our ignorance and karma, to reveal to us the innate Divinity within ourselves and awaken our inner fire. Once awakened as the inner fire, we begin to understand our own highest wisdom as our Guru and the inner Guru.

Heart song - Every one of us is gifted with a heart song that plays and sometimes, in our stillness, we listen to this song and contribute to this song and we then become this heart song. Sages who are in silence and deep meditation often write in poetic form since they have delved into their own heart song and their mind is flowing from this state of joy.

Himalayan limitations - Each of us is born with our own limits and these unique limits of ours are like the mountain; the biggest of our limitations is therefore like the Himalayas. However, we are Spirit, and we can fly over them, as swans do. The swan referred to by the Yogi is our own higher conscious mind-state.

Human love form - After attaining the joys of bliss, the Yogi then manifests that ecstatic state of being in all realities including the body. Our Siddhar Sages say: after attaining the knowing of God as bliss, become the bliss form and acquire a love body, the body of bliss.

Inner lamp - In the Yogic path, we understand the most empowering grace to be that of stillness that comes from having our 'inner lamp' lit. This inner lamp is located at the root chakra. When the inner lamp is lit, we experience undiluted joy and happiness and we set Yogic disciplines to expand this state of joy to grow the inner fires.

Kundalini fire - The inner fire is also the Kundalini fire that is awake through worship of the Divine, through meditation and through Yogic techniques. Chanting, singing, dancing and any other joyful activity with singular focus of the Divine awakens the Kundalini fire.

Laxmi – Goddess Laxmi is the feminine facet of Lord Vishnu, the God of sustenance, nurturing and abundance. When we understand our own mind as awake, we awaken to Consciousness that is abundant in material and spiritual wealth. The feminine Divinity of an awakened mind of higher Consciousness (there is a masculine and feminine aspect of every facet of the Divine) is Goddess Laxmi, who has the attributes of magnificence, inspiration, fulfillment, fame, family, genius, power, love, wisdom and all positive attributes we may seek in life. Goddess Laxmi is represented as the heart chakra in bloom.

Lingam - The most perfect symbol depicting Infinity is the shape of a Lingam. A Yogi brings all the focus, energy of enthusiasm and singular intent to invoke Lord Siva, the power of Infinity through a Lingam that then represents Infinity. The Lingam acquires the vibrancy of the invoked presence, while the Yogi is blessed with the growing energies of the Divine Presence invoked in the Lingam. Beyond this description comes the brahmanical explanation of a Lingam being a representation of the male genital and the base that holds the Lingam as the female organ, the Yoni – to depict the union of male and female and the fires of the sacred union.

Mantra - A mantra is the sacred resonance of Consciousness embedded with energies of all those who chanted before it and are given by the Guru to the disciple as blessings of Consciousness.

Mother Kundalini - While there are several books on this subject, Nandhiji seeks to address Mother Kundalini as expressed in the experience of the inner fire that rises up like a cobra from the root chakra all the way above our crown chakra. Mother Kundalini is another state of Consciousness that is of Divine origin.

Mulam - Mulam means the center, the root, foundation and the Source. The mulam is the epicenter of the root chakra.

Muladara - Muladhara is the root chakra. The root chakra is vital in our spiritual and material realities. In the Siddhar traditions, the muladhara as Lord Ganesh is very important as it is from the muladhara that the inner fires begin. Once again, it is from the muladhara that the inner fire can be enhanced and grown so it blossoms through each of the chakras above.

Nada - In the biblical expression of the Divine, Genesis begins with: 'In the beginning was the Word. The Word was with God and the Word was God.' This Word is the resonance vibration, the nada. The universe is made up of vibrations, as is infinity and vibrations can be experienced through the nada and expressed by way of the mantra that carries nada. Within nada is Consciousness.

Nataraja, The Dancing Siva - The infinity of the cosmos as taught by the Yogis is perfectly in tune with modern science, as demonstrated by the vastness of space within the atom. A Yogi realizes this vastness and the world within the smallest within the minutest, as the perpetual Dance. This Dance is of Oneness, who is revered by the Yogis as Lord Siva.

Navrathri - These are nine nights based on the lunar calendar when the Goddess in all her forms is celebrated and invoked. Invoking the Goddess leads us to enlightenment, as this grace completes us in every possible way.

Primal Harmony - When in the grace of Yogic union, the undiluted bliss of ananda is the primal Harmony state where the mind has ceased and is guided by bliss through awareness.

Primal nada - In the innermost silence within, is cosmic resonance. This is like the resonance we experience when we listen to the echoing sound of a shell placed near our ears - the sound of nothingness that contains the universe. It is from this infinite space that the AUM as a resonance has been expressed by the Yogis as the primal nada. In this primal resonance is the blissful dance of stillness - as the inner music, the heart song.

Primal thread - In the state where the mind has given way to the thoughtless, mindless void mind, we are guided by awareness. This awareness is a primal thread of Consciousness. Sometimes, even as a child we innately know or even in our day-to-day activities, we are intuitively guided.

This is the primal thread of Consciousness that we connect with from our previous births, our connection with Divine Beings who guide us, and our connection with our own innate awakened being within.

Puja - A puja is the mother of all meditation. A puja is the worship of the Divine performed with a super-alert mind, aligning every thought to the Divine with offerings through mantra and in the physical, with flowers, water and so on. When a puja is done, we are invoking the presence of the Deity and the blessings of fulfillment of the intent within the puja (if any). From the Yogic experience, a puja dissolves the mind, breaks and dissolves away clutter and previous thought momentum, and leads us to a state of clarity and Harmony. A puja easily leads us to a perpetual meditative state, that works alongside our daily activity - in other words, after the puja we are in a meditative state no matter what we do.

Sacred fires – During the Yogic experience, each activity is seen as a burst of energy as if a fire has been lit. For instance, there is a fire happening in the digestive tract, there is the fire that happens when we think and there are the external fires that are lit to invoke the Divine. The fire is a perfect medium used by humanity through the ages of history and in every culture around the world to invoke the Divine. When Yogis invoke the Divine through fire, sacredness is the outcome, and it transforms the Yogi, the Yogi's thoughts and the world; Source presence of Divine energies is brought into human realities through the fire.

Sages - Acquiring the higher conscious mind, to be beyond the mind as Spirit having the human experience, we are the Sages, journeying beyond Consciousness through each breath.

Samadhi - The realization of intense joy, for example when the Divine, the mind and the five senses unite, and are absorbed by the Divine. In samadhi, even if breathing has slowed or sometimes stopped, the inner fire is lit and the

Divine pranic energies keep the Yogi alive. States of samadhi lead to higher and higher levels of Consciousness. For a Yogi, the bridge to the Divine is through samadhi, a connection that that yields the timelessness, the stillness and the ecstatic states of joy to be One. After a samadhi experience, the mind is transformed, having climbed several notches above as blessings to be evolved.

Shrine - Within all places of worship resides the Sanctum Sanctorum, the shrine in which is housed the Divine. After deep intense focus, the awareness of ourselves being the dweller of the shrine emerges as from our own center of centers. Yogis undertake enormous pilgrimages to various shrines to then go within their own shrine and invoke the Divinity of all Shrines.

Siddhi - As we journey within, our mind becomes subdued together with other facets of our mind that we never knew we had. We begin to be aware of the 'sixth' sense. We begin to wake up to our own inner genius. We start realizing the super-normal things that happen around us. This is Siddhi. For a Yogi, most siddhis are distractions, particularly if too much attention is paid to them as they attract karmic limitations. Karma always holds us back from being the Infinite. The Siddhar Yogis utilize certain siddhis however, to deepen their spiritual practices - like utilizing the outer body experience to visit the sacred Sanctum Sanctorum of Temples. In turn, Siddhars avoid any siddhi that can lead them astray or gather karma - like fortune telling for someone or forcing an external circumstance to bend for a personal need. Siddhis used to enhance dharma for humanity are the best application to further grace on the inner journey. Otherwise, it is best to avoid acquiring siddhis.

Siva - Lord Siva (pronounced in northern India as Lord Shiva) from the perspective of Yogic wisdom is the vastness of infinity, as in the sound 'Seee' and the experience of joy, bliss and dynamic stillness of the Goddess energies as 'Vaaa'. The ultimate Oneness of Source/God in the Yogic traditions of the Siddhars is Lord Siva. Lord Siva is the experience of our own vast Spirit and the infinity of the cosmic as the God, the Almighty Infinity.

Swan - When awakened to the understanding that there is wisdom beyond our own thinking ability and the mind, we begin to understand higher Consciousness as that of the swan. The mythical swan could drink the milk content separately out of water i.e., a Yogi could perceive only the right thought and action through whatever way reality presents itself. Great Sages are called Parama Hamsa - the Great Swans – as they have attained the wisdom of Consciousness.

Tantiram and Tantra - The Spirit we experience is the vastness of our own self and the human experience of the Spirit is the Yogic union that is tantra. The weaving of the Spirit with the human to experience the state of orgasmic joy for a Yogi is to expand this state of bliss and joy to all levels and layers of awareness and realities. What is experienced as the flash of orgasmic joy as in sexual orgasm holds the vast eternal everlasting orgasm continued through each breath, every moment, and appreciated through all realities of the human experience. This is tantra. The roots to the wisdom of tantra is Tantiram which entails the wholeness of the human to evolve, in order to become the Angelic Being, the Yogi.

Tapas - The inner fire lit, is the beginning of tapas. Tapas is the effort, time, focus and involvement within the inner fire through mantra recitation, meditation and awareness. When in tapas, we are clearing away the past imprints of karma that contain and limit us. In tapas, we are invoking the Divine presence to be our inner fire to journey through Consciousness. Tapas is much like cooking the Divine with time, patience and devotional love.

Timelessness - Attaining the single focus that is characterized by intense bliss, we step into timelessness. With more practice and immersion in this timelessness, when a Yogi emerges back into human realities, reality is understood as time that is defined through the timelessness of being.

Tummo - The tummo is an advanced Yogic insight to awaken the inner lamp to keep the body warm and in balance, irrespective of extreme cold or heat. The tummo wisdom comes from the mystical end of the Yogic path. In Tibetan Tantric Buddhism, the aspirant who has attained the tummo wisdom is led to a frozen lake on a cold windy night, clad in only a cotton robe. This cotton robe is soaked in cold water and worn by the monk. Through the night, the monk is able to dry several wet cotton robes. Those who are able to do this are called the 'Repa', the cotton clad ones.

Turiya - Beyond the states of being awake, dreaming and sleep, is the higher conscious state of mind called Turiya, a deep meditation. In this state, there is a rapid expansion in Consciousness and closeness to Source. Thoughts from the Turiya state of mind are potent and are easily manifested; super-normal thoughts are likely to spring from this state as inner genius. The state of Turiya naturally unfolds for anyone in the depth of prayer, meditation or inspired work and play.

Vibrancy - In the beginning and in the end, energy and matter are vibrations. Consciousness is also energy. Through the mantra, vibrations are transferred. A Yogi attains inner vibrancy and is able to transfer this vibrancy as Consciousness to all, directly through the mantras and teachings, and indirectly, by simply being a presence.

Vishnu - When the mind is awake, aware and connected to be one with Source, we are the 'Knower', denoted by the ancient Tamil word, 'Ari'. It is from the word 'Ari' that Lord Vishnu derives the word Hari. From the Yogic perspective, all our wisdom and knowing comes from experience. So, when we experience ourselves as the vastness of Spirit, the Supreme Self, we are experiencing Lord Siva. The awake mind that celebrated the Divine is Lord Visnu - the mind that sustains and guides us.

Void - When we journey within our mind to reach the no-mind state where we experience the void, we understand this void to be empowering Source energies that hold stillness within the dance of joy and bliss. It is for this reason that the vastness of infinity/space is represented as the Dancing Lord Siva.

Yantra - There is a perfect Divine form in all the realities we perceive. The Yogis relate Source in physical form through the diagrammatic representation of the yantra. Each Divine facet is unique and represented as a yantra based on the energy involved. Any form created to contain Source in a pattern is a yantra. A group of Divine people with focus on the Divine could be a human yantra.

Yogi - Anyone lit within and following the discipline to tend and grow the inner fire through any method to gain higher Consciousness, stillness and joyful union with Source is a Yogi.

Yogic unity - Yoga is to unite with Source. In Yogic unity, the human mind unites with the cosmic infinite wisdom; this leads to absorption within, in the state of 'samadhi', where the external senses have shut down and we are one with the Divine. Experiencing the Yogic unity, each breath, each thought and each moment is guided and is a meditation into itself.

For Nandhiji, all the wisdom of awakening, guidance and the spiritual journey is the grace of his Gurus. Each Guru opened a threshold of Consciousness and aligned Nandhiji to the grace of the lineage of Light, Prayers and Purpose as the ancient intent.

Nandhiji's Gurus	
	**Bhairava Sekarswamy:** He took Nandhiji through the awakening death experience. Bhairava Sekarswamy set Nandhiji on the path of a Yogi by kindling the inner fire of bliss and joy through this initiation. This awakening to the inner fire led Nandhiji into the inner journeys of uncovering more and more of bliss as a Yogi seeking the expanding Consciousness. Bhairava Sekarswamy continues his own

	deep spiritual practice and several dharma works such as feeding the pilgrims every full moon night, taking care of animals, especially dogs among other activities.
Saddhu Krishnaveni Amma, the lady saint who meditated for over 65 years in her cave in Kalyana Thirtham, South India. It is hard to imagine how this saint lived all by herself in a cave that is today a tiger sanctuary. After years of daily rigorous meditative discipline, Nandhiji's external realities, including the business Nandhiji had; his family; his home-everything simply dissolved away. When Nandhiji's parents and friends became worried that Nandhiji would now leave the human external realities and go to the long solitudes of the caves,	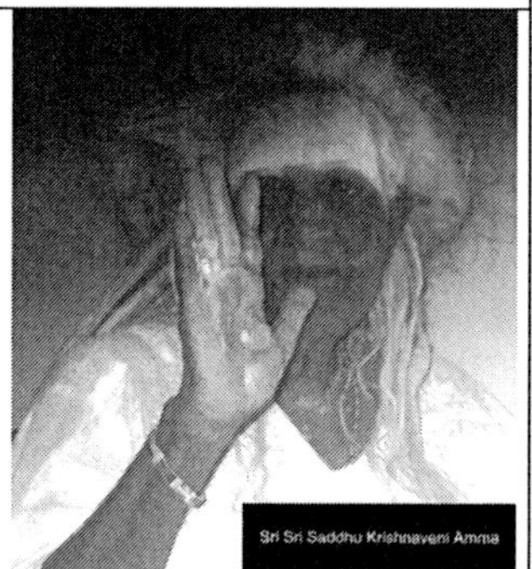 Sri Sri Saddhu Krishnaveni Amma

Saddhu Krishnaveni Amma took the reins over the spiritual guidance of Nandhiji. She directed Nandhiji to the next chapter in his life- a life of a Yogi householder. Saddhu Krishnaveni Amma left her body in 2011 April.	
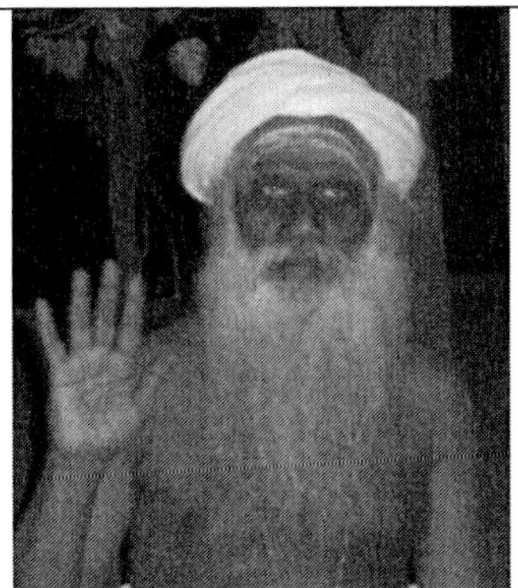	**Siddhar Rajaswamy** opened the mystical doors of Siddhar tradition to Nandhiji just after Saddhu Krishnaveni Amma took Nandhiji into her fold. Siddhar Guru Rajaswamy connects his ancient lineage of the Siddhars with Nandhiji. Siddhar Rajaswamy is a living master carrying the traditions going back to Siddhar Bhoganathar. His powerful teaching is in the example doing constant service for the society- feeding the hungry, looking after

	the tribals, re-instating old temples etc. His daily prayers and fire rituals are for uplifting humanity as Consciousness. One of Siddhar Rajaswamy's teachings is- by invoking the Divine Masters and serving the intent of Consciousness, we become the Master. www.siddhar.net
Amma, Mother Amritandamayi, (The Hugging Saint) woke Nandhiji to a life purpose. When Nandhiji was a saddhu (a renunciate seeker) he had met Amma and told her of his childhood dream of saving the life of old cows. Amma set Nandhiji back into the human realities with the knowing of his purpose, with a simple but incredibly power-packed directive: 'Just do it!' Almost immediately after, Nandhiji saw realities that would bring him to Santa Monica, California to work on his life dream and vision that unfolds now, as in the	

Declaration of Consciousness and the Ariven Vision. www.amma.org	
	**Siddhapurush Babaji Baba Nataraj** is a humble master who walked the length and breadth across USA several times, as a pilgrimage. His radiant presence of Harmony is such that wild birds sit on him unafraid. He has been Nandhiji's Guru in Santa Monica, guiding, teaching and unveiling for Nandhiji the deep thresholds of Consciousness. He shared his sacred space with Nandhiji every Thursday for many years. His website: www.siva-mandir.wix.com/baba-nataraja

Siddhar Mahasivaswamy lived over 35 years in solitude in the forest of Nambi Hills. Siddhar Mahasivaswamy mentored Nandhiji through advanced Yogic techniques and meditation. Siddhar Mahasivaswamy appointed Nandhiji as the custodian of his lineage. Siddhar Mahasivaswamy left his body 2011, April He was an amazing mystic who would spend hours together meditating the tiger sanctuary forest area in solitude.	

	**Siddhar Guru Ayya Narayana** is the Siddhar Sage who meditated for 18 years atop the sacred mountain of Thiruvannamalai, drinking just a cup of milk each day and not moving while sitting in one single position. He continues to attain one of humanity's most powerful meditations in the quiet of his secluded village near Kanyakumari. He ventures out of his meditative solitude once a day to bless the few who seek his spiritual guiding grace. As a living Master, Ayya is one of the major custodians of humanity's Consciousness as he continues to mediate. Ayya continues to guide Nandhiji through the mastery of the inner realm and the external realm of purpose.

Ariven Temple Three Visions of Nandhiji:

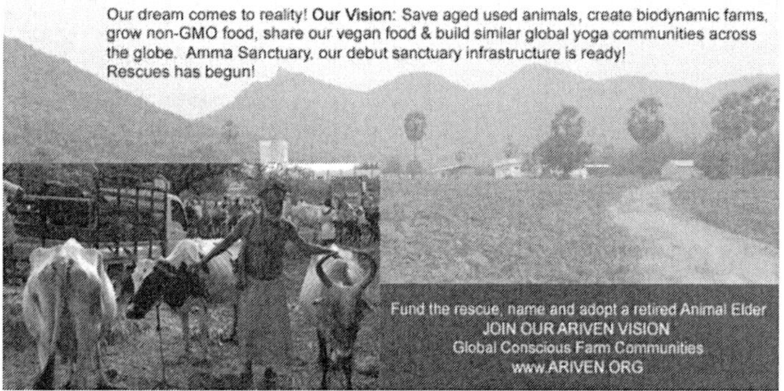

This is Nandhiji's childhood aspiration- to save the life of cows and oxen taken to the slaughter-house; create farms to utilize the droppings of these animals to grow organic food; to feed hundreds of thousands of hungry and poor. This Vision now is in motion as the Ariven Community with our first sanctuary Amma Sanctuary started with our intent- to have thousands of similar sanctuaries across the globe saving hundreds of thousands of aged retired farm animals; create vast biodynamic farms to grow non-GMO, intelligent food to address global hunger and the curse of Monsanto; develop yoga communities with each of these centers. The net effect of this vision would further the collective goodness of humanity as in compassion, love, sharing and as global family of Oneness. www.ariven.org

Nandhiji envisioned a day the world would unite with yoga and all who practiced yoga would realize to attain Consciousness. In 2003 we trademarked World Yoga Day and prayed that this intent of mine would come true. In 2014 Prime Minister Narendra Modiji announced in the United Nations my dream- a day for yoga globally. Later, the Indian government approached us for our rights and we requested that they consider Mahasivratri, the time observed by all Hindus over the ages, a time aligned to attainment enlightenment. The Indian government mentioned that they had the date already fixed and planned in the United Nations. So, instead of confrontation we chose to compliment the initiative by India's Yogi leader, Modiji, by changing our vision to World Yogi Day.

Through yoga, we attain the highest aspiration of the human, to be the Yogi! www.worldyogiday.org

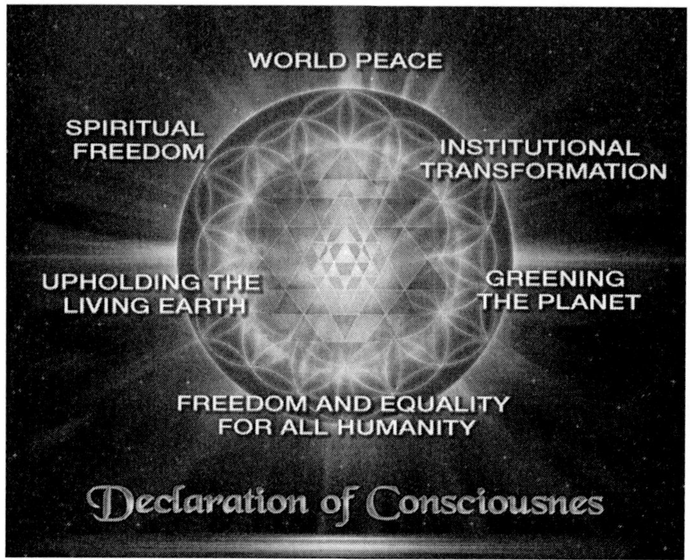

Our larger vision for humanity is the Declaration of Consciousness Movement:

Story behind Declaration of Consciousness Movement:

Nandhiji first landed in USA nine days before September 11th 2001. The terrorist attack in the name of 'God' shocked him. Four years later, he conducted the opening fire ceremony for Bhakti Fest, one of the large yoga festivals of USA, on Sept 11. To commemorate the Opening Ceremony of Bhakti Fest, Nandhiji had the gathering chant the name 'Allah', a collective prayer to seek the solution for this madness through Source/God. Instead of hate, Nandhiji thought love was the solution. In 2012, Bhakti Fest, the vision of the Declaration of Consciousness was birthed by Nandhiji. Consciousness is the only answer to bring our world to sanity, coexistence, unity, understanding and peace. Declaration of Consciousness

Movement is a global phenomena that suggests all Nations to adopt its principles as the intrinsic inherent right of every human across cultures, religion, gender and beliefs.

What if nations set the intent of Consciousness for its people as basics of tenets ie, Nonviolence; Women's equality, Children, Elders, Ethical Commerce, spiritual freedom, Mother Earth etc. as norms that was beyond religion or rather, the true essence of all religions in varied degrees.

In Consciousness, religions, establishments, organizations, societies and individuals will need upgrades to be causal of Peace. While we envision majority of nations adopt the Declaration of Consciousness, we are building an Online Grid as the foundation to support, nurture and spread the grass root movement.

Nine Principles of Declaration of Consciousness

1. NON-VIOLENCE / AHIMSA / CAUSE NO HARM
2. EQUALITY
3. WOMEN'S RIGHTS
4. FREEDOM
5. CHILDREN'S WELLBEING
6. HONOURING OUR ELDERS
7. CONSCIOUS ORGANISATIONS
8. MOTHER EARTH
9. UNITY

SIGN the Declaration of Consciousness:
www.SignDc.org

Cover Art: painting by Nandhiji Siddha Darsanam Art Gallery www.nandhiji.com

The cover says Awakening of the Inner Guru, which is the Inner Prophet. So, who are they? We each have 5 Gurus. The first is our left and right Breath, second is our Mother and Father, third is the Gurus who open doors of Source God to us, the fourth is the awakening of our Inner Guru that is Tapas (often mentioned in the book as Kundalini fire) and the fifth Guru is the realization of every experience and everything as a Guru.